SONNING COMMON PRIMARY SCHOOL

A History 1913 – 2013

Melanie White

To Rory and Lola,

Melanie White
09.01.2013

Sonning Common Primary School
A History
1913 – 2013

Melanie White

Edition one, published in 2012 by Sonning Common Primary School

ISBN 978-0-9574663-0-2

Copyright © Melanie White

Designed and typeset by 2d Solutions Ltd. London
Printed by Breckland Print, Norfolk

Contents

Foreword

I am delighted to contribute a Foreword to this remarkable book. Melanie White has painstakingly sifted through a hundred years' worth of evidence with dedication and skill. The result is a full and interesting account from the opening of the school in 1913, through two World Wars to the technological age we live in, the local children shining through every chapter of the story. The publishing of this book sets the stage for the Centenary Celebrations planned for 2013.

On behalf of the Governors I would like to thank Melanie for her very hard work and to congratulate her on her achievement. This history of Sonning Common Primary School will delight her readers and be treasured as a souvenir of the Centenary Year.

Mrs Jackie Million, Chair of Governors.

Chapter One
Education in Sonning Common before 1913

There was no school in Sonning Common before 1913. Children from Sonning Common attended Kidmore End School (from 1856), Peppard School or Eye and Dunsden School, probably depending which was closest to their home. For example, Eva Prior (born 1907) lived in Grove Road from the age of 4 and is recorded as *'a frail child who had to be pushed in a handcart to Kidmore End school every day'* (she later attended Sonning Common School and there is a photograph of her from 1915 in the next chapter).

There were a number of key pieces of legislation prior to the decision to build a new school. The Forster Elementary Education Act 1870 required partially state-funded Board Schools to be set up to provide elementary (primary) education in areas where existing provision was inadequate. Board schools were managed by elected school boards. The schools were able to charge a fee for attendance.

The Elementary Education Act 1880 insisted on compulsory attendance from 5–10 years although the purpose of compulsory education was (and still is) hotly debated. For poorer families, ensuring their children attended school proved difficult, as it was more tempting to send them out to work if the opportunity to earn an extra income was available. Thirteen years later the Elementary Education (School Attendance) Act 1893 came into force which raised the minimum leaving age to 11 and in 1899 the school leaving age was raised to 12 years.

The Free Education Act 1891 provided for the state payment of school fees up to ten shillings per week and the Balfour Act of 1902 abolished School Boards and replaced them with Local Education Authorities (L.E.A.s). The Fisher Education Act of 1918 set the school leaving age at 14 without exception whilst L.E.A.s could set it at 15 years if they chose.

Thus the need was established for a school in Sonning Common. These schools were generally called Council Schools and had 6 managers who appointed staff. Sonning Common had no parish council of its own thus explaining the naming of the school Eye and Dunsden Sonning Common School.

The first meeting of the school managers was held on November 12th 1912 with Revd H. Eric Robson elected chairman. The other managers were Miss Maitland, Mr Cox, Mr Holland, Mr Pound and Mr Sacret. Mr John Giles was appointed as caretaker on a salary of £10 per annum.

The cost of the original buildings was recorded in the managers' minutes. Briefly, the total cost including furniture and fittings was £3450, £865 was paid immediately with the balance £2585 to be paid by June 1962 – this must have seemed a long term loan indeed.

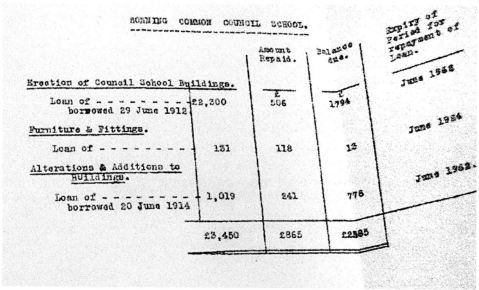

Extract from Managers' Minute Book

Chapter Two
Mr F. W. Woodward (1913 – 1922)

In November 1912, three candidates for Headmaster were interviewed (all with a wife who would be the second member of staff). Mr Frederick W. Woodward and Mrs Florence Woodward were appointed and would live in the school house as subsequent headteachers did for the next fifty years. Mr Woodward's salary was £115 per annum and his wife's £51. On January 29th 1913, a supplementary teacher, Miss Minnie Heath, was appointed. By 1914 the head's salary had increased to £150 but when, in 1916, Mr and Mrs Woodward requested that both salaries be increased by £10, he was granted £5 and Mrs Woodward, nothing. Assistant staff turnover was fairly rapid in the early days of the school. A Miss G. Woodward was appointed, though it is unclear whether she was a relative of the headmaster. By April 1916 she had resigned and was replaced by Miss Porter on a salary of £35 per annum. In August Miss Heath resigned and Miss Cox was appointed alongside Dorothy Callis as a monitress with a view to becoming a pupil teacher – salary £8. In 1919 Winifred Callis became a monitress and was later, in 1920, accepted as a pupil teacher. Winnie appears as a pupil in a 1915 photograph.

Staff 1920

Opening Day

Fifty bills were posted in the school radius announcing the opening date and inviting visits. The Eye and Dunsden Sonning Common Council School opened on January 6th 1913 with 69 children admitted. By July 1913 the school was already oversubscribed with 84 children on roll and 19 waiting to be given a place. On June 16th when the managers visited they declared:

> 'all seats taken by pupils'.

The managers wrote immediately to the Education Secretary requesting a doubling of the premises.

The school was divided into 'mixed' and 'infants'. The first child on roll was Nellie Grimshaw (D.O.B. 03/11/03), aged 9.

Date of Admission (or Re-Admission).			FULL NAME OF CHILD.	NAME OF PARENT OR GUARDIAN.	ADDRESS.
Day.	Mon.	Year.			
6	1	13	Grimshaw Nellie	Grimshaw Mr John	Shiplake Bottom S.
6	1	13	Keats Helen Grace	Keats William	High Street Shiplake Bottom
6	1	13	Keats Rose Winifr	Keats William	"
6	1	13	Garrett Wilfred	Garrett Thomas	Chalk Hou Gros Ke
6	1	13	Garrett Evelyn	"	"
6	1	13	Garrett Alfred	"	"
6	1	13	Josey Henry Albert	Josey Albert	Home Wor Son
6	1	13	Huggins Mabel Mary	Huggins Frederick	Grns Rd Sonning
6	1	13	Huggins Florence Jane	"	"
6	1	13	Prior Amy	Prior James	Grns Rd Sonning
6	1	13	Prior Eva	"	"
6	1	13	Pound Elsie	Pound John	Oakfield Sonning
6	1	13	Pound Sidney	"	"
6	1	13	Gillett James William	Gillett James	The Retreat Sonning
6	1	13	Gillett Frederic Thomas	"	"
6	1	13	Bacon Frances Louise	Bacon Francis Har	2 Manor Cottage S
6	1	13	Horton Thomas Edward	Horton Thomas	White Hou S

First page of the Admissions Book

The school was surrounded by a fence. Boys and girls were not allowed to mix at break times and a fence clearly marked their respective areas. There were also separate entrances for boys and girls and the toilets for pupils were outside, the only indoor toilet being for the exclusive use of the staff.

Playground 1913

Grove Road 1913 – now library frontage

The buildings are barely changed today although over the years there have been additions and extensions. The roof of the original building (on Grove Road) is divided into three sections. The gabled area in the centre formed the original building and the two parts on either side are the first extensions. As well as the outside toilets there were attached sheds, the School House and the building behind the School House which now has an entrance onto the car park (originally the school garden). This was the cookery room and not attached to the rest of the junior block as it is today. The cookery room was staffed by a teacher who cycled from Nettlebed three days a week and the room was also used by different local schools. On the other days of the week it was used as a *'babies room'*.

By the end of 1913, the caretaker had resigned despite additional payments for some *'unpleasant tasks'* which he was called on to perform –

> *'The managers recommend that a sum of 2/6 (12.5p) be paid
> to the caretaker for pumping out the sewage from the cesspit'.*

By September 1914 the new buildings were ready for occupation and the 107 pupils on roll were divided into 4 groups by age: 5 year olds, 6 – 7 year olds, 8 – 9 year olds and 10 – 13 year olds. As agreed, the upper part of each inner wall was made of glass so that the headmaster could see from one end of his school to the other.

In December 1919 there was a request for the school buildings to be used for dances when not being used by pupils. This gave the managers a dilemma – who would pay for any damage? It was eventually agreed that the school rooms could be hired with a charge of £1 for an evening, including lighting (no electricity at this stage) but any resulting damage must be paid for. If heating was required, the organisers must bring their own fuel!

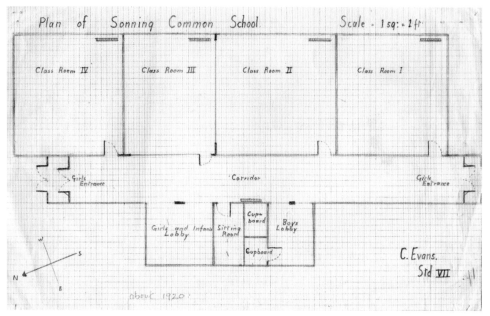

Plan of the school drawn by C. Evans approx 1920 – the entrance on the right should read 'boys entrance'

The boys and girls in 1915 were photographed separately, of course.

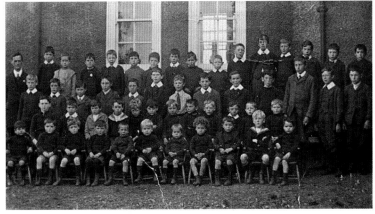

Boys 1915

Back row (names remembered): Mr Woodward, ? Turner, Alec Callis, Henry Josey, ? Richardson, George Hoadley, George Smith, Frank Brewer, Don Brind
Next row: Ron Brewer, Tom Pigden, Will Allwright, Eric Poole, Billy Leadbetter, Will Brewer
Next row: Harry Cobb, John Allwright, Charlie Allaway, Tom Huggins, Bert Cox, John Freeman, Ted Cox
Front row: Maurice Pigden, Charlie Paddick, Jack Castle, Jack Batting

Girls 1915

Back row (names remembered): Emily Pigden, Elsie Pound, Olive Ilsley, Win Stevens, Ada Smith, Mabel Huggins, Chris Richardson
Next row: Ena Collins, Annie Illsley, Eva Prior, Floss Huggins, Eva Brind, Lucy Witchelow
Next row: Miss Heath, Winnie Smith, ? Batting, Ethel James, Dorothy Glade, Gwen Cook, Winnie Callis, Muriel Cox, Helen Josey, Mrs Woodward, Miss Woodward
Next row: Gwen Godfrey, Doris Huggins, Gwen Clay, Elsie Turner, Dorothy Webb, Eileen Hoadley, Kath Josey
Next row: Nina Roberts, Audrey Howes, Phyliss Callis, Emily Allwright, Alice James, Nora Smith, Annie Witchelow, Gwen Taylor, Esme Paddick, Dorothy Leadbetter

And in 1920, together.

Group 1 1920

Back row: Percy Novell, Bert Cox, George Smith, Tom Pigden, Bill Allwright, Lewis Turner, George Costin, Frank Hermon
Second row: Audrey Howes, Floss Huggins, Henry Josey, ?, Fred Ball, Tom Huggins, Kathleen Josey, May Pitt
Front row: Edie Harris, Winnie Norris, Rene Lawrence, Dorothy Bunwell, Phyliss Pigden, Dorothy Leadbetter, Eva Prior, Flo Bunwell, Nora Smith, Annie Ilsley, Dorothy Webb

Group 2, 1920

Back row: Eileen Hoadley, Gwen Taylor, Clara Cobb, Emily Allwright, Phyllis Pigden, Alice James, Emily Turner, Amy Ball, Annie Witchelow
Second row: George Varndell, George Pope, Ted Wells, Ted Cox, Ted Summers, ?, Phyllis Costin, Clarence Ferris, George Smith, Joe Lucas, Fred Richardson
Third row: Lionel Lucas?, Bert White, Charlie Paddick, Doris Huggins, Gwen Godfrey, Esme Paddick, Miss Tester, Gwennie Clay, Evelyn Cox, Win Hoadley, Elsie Snow, Doris Randall
Front row: Ken Wright, Maurice Pigden, Ted Wells, Charlie Allaway, ?, Leslie Digby-Smith, Ronald Long, Lionel Lucas?

The 5 years old class in 1920

Back row: Bert Randall, Anthony Richardson, Margaret Atherton, ?, Miss Martin, Iris Batting, Freda Gunston, Bob Callis, ?, Queenie Wells
Front row: Robert Adams, Brenda Howes, ?, Iris Summers, Sybil Ball, ?, Charlie Harris, Aubrey Gunston, Eric Roberts

Most of the names for these photographs were supplied at least 25 years ago by Margaret Atherton (third left, top row) who became Mrs Redding and were collected by B.M. Brown.

There are examples of pupils' work still available to look at today –

WRITING. Date 6 . 7 . 21

Third Term

Composition

A half holiday in Summer

When we came to school last Friday morning, we were told that we could have a half holiday because we had worked hard on Thursday, when the inspector came. When we set off home we arranged to have a cricket match on Peppard Common at 2.o.clock About half past one I set off up to the Common and arrived there at the time appointed.

The rival captains soon tossed up and our side went in first At first we made a very bad start three wickets falling talh for forty three runs, but we soon pulled the game together and were all out for ninety six runs.

Then the other side went in and they scored seventy four with the loss of nine wickets. With only one wicket in hand they were in a bad position to get a victory, for the last man got bowled for six runs.

After they were out, we started our second innings and scored eighty nine, but they were all out for thirty seven. When we had finished, some of them went home and we had a game among ourselves for an hour and, half.

Thomas Wheatley's writing 06/07/21 when he was aged 12 years

George Varndell appears in the 1920 (Group 2) photograph page 8.

In Appendix 1 you will see examples of the examinations pupils had to pass in 1921 in order to win a scholarship to Henley Grammar school.

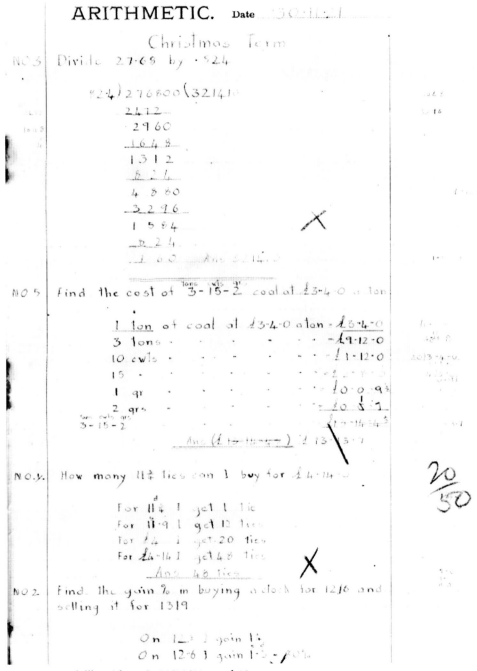

George Varndell's arithmetic 30/11/21, aged 12 years

Sport

Here is the 1920 football team.

Punishment

It was not long before the first corporal punishment was administered – as far as we know these were all recorded in the punishment book which was maintained by the headmaster and scrutinised and signed regularly by the school managers. Exactly one week after the school opened – on 13th January – Jessie Moore received one stroke for disobedience. This, one assumes, was a female pupil and the second pupil named in the book, Lucy Witchelow certainly demonstrates that girls were not exempt from physical punishment. Lucy appears in the girls' photograph of 1915.

Punishment Book cover and first entries

Health

On 2nd March 1915 came the first exclusion for 'verminous heads' but this was a common occurrence and hardly worth a mention. In 1917 the school was closed for 2 days for spotted fever and in January 1918 for 8 and a half weeks until March 18th for an outbreak of whooping cough.

On 19th November 1918 the school was closed for the rest of the term due to the influenza epidemic which affected the whole country at the end of World War 1. It is estimated that up to 250,000 people died in Britain and as many (or more) than 50 million worldwide in a pandemic that lasted for 2 years.

Trips, visits and gifts

Boys were taken on trips to local farms and in March 1915 Mr Woodward proposed a Flower Show for pupils. Here are the school gardeners in 1920.

Older pupils were taken on nature rambles and there were visits to Emmer Green Brick Works, Huntley and Palmers Biscuit Factory, the Abbey ruins and the Forbury gardens in Reading. All trips had to be sanctioned by the Education Authority and agreed by the managers of the school.

OXFORDSHIRE EDUCATION COMMITTEE.

Application for permission to take scholars to places of educational interest
under Article 44 (b) of the code for Elementary Schools.

August 15 ____1913.

Name of School.	Date and time of proposed visit.	Number and standard (or class) of children.	Place or places to be visited.	Names of Teachers accompanying the scholars.
Eye & Dunsden Sonning Common Council School	Oct: 23. 1913. (1.40 - 3.40)	Class I + II 15	Emmer Green Brick Works	
	March. 18. 1914 (10 a.m - 12. a.m)	14	Huntley + Palmers Biscuit factory. Reading	Woodward. Frederick William
	March. 18. (1.40. - 3.40)	"	Forbury Gardens & Reading abbey Ruins	
	May. 20. 1914. (1.40 - 3.40)	14	Suttons Trial Grounds Reading	
	July. 15. 1914. (1.40 - 3.40)	15	Reading Museum	

Object of the Visit :

1. To give the children some idea of the manufactures + industries carried on in the district

2. By visiting Museum + ruins to help them to get a better idea of history.

J. W. Woodward. Head Teacher.

Approved on behalf of the Education Committee.

F. Elford
26/8/13
Education Secretary.

Approved on behalf of the Board of Education.

Application for permission to take pupils on a trip - 1913

From 1913, the managers each gave five shillings per year to be used at the headteacher's discretion to provide prizes for progress and proficiency.

Music was always important in the school and in July 1913 a piano was given *'absolutely'* by Lady Margaret Crichton-Maitland in order for pupils to learn appropriate songs and hymns.

World War 1

Mr Woodward was passed fit for general service in September 1916 and was called up for military service.

On November 9th 1916 the managers wrote to Mr Woodward:

> Dear Sir,
> At a meeting of the Managers held on November 9th it was their unanimous desire to express to you their appreciation of all the excellent work you have done for the school.
>
> The Managers very much regret your enforced absence, which they hope will not be of long duration, and they very much look forward to the time when you will be able to resume the duties of Head-master.
>
> Yours truly,
> E. S. Craig (correspondent)

In his absence, Mrs Woodward took the role of Headteacher although she was not entitled to her husband's salary. The war did not affect the school greatly although cookery lessons ceased in 1917 because of food shortages. Pupils probably enjoyed their half day holidays to pick blackberries so that jam could be made for the Army and Navy.

Mr Woodward returned safely to his post after the war. The school by this time had 160 children and five teachers.

Mr and Mrs Woodward remained for a further 4 years. They resigned in January 1922 and Mr and Mrs Forder were invited for interview.

Chapter Three
Mr P. Forder (1922 – 1947)

$\mathcal{M}$r Philip Forder and his wife, Edith took charge of the school in 1922 when the Woodwards departed. No photographs of him have come to light but he is described by a former pupil as always wearing a suit, having a little moustache and always with a handkerchief up his sleeve. Other members of staff were Mrs Forder, Miss Tester and Mrs Clayton. During this time, Sonning Common began to grow and the area was described as *'a growing district with more younger than older scholars'*. New members of staff were appointed in 1927: Miss Higgins, an uncertificated teacher, and Ronald Britnell, a student teacher for one year. On the resignation of Miss Tester, a Mrs Jones was appointed.

National changes in education included the 1921 Fisher Education Act which raised the school leaving age to 14 and the Hadow Report in 1926 recommending the abolition of Elementary Schools covering the age groups 5 -14, in favour of Primary and Secondary education. This was not to happen for some time in Sonning Common but there were opportunities for the more able pupils to attend other schools, a move not entirely to Mr Forder's liking. In July 1929 he reported that two female pupils had been successful in the County Junior Scholarship examination (for Henley Grammar School) and a further 7 pupils recommended to Reading Central schools. This would leave only 33 children over the age of eleven. The managers wrote as follows to the Education committee:

'In view of the good work done in the past by the headmaster and staff of the school, the managers strongly protest against the policy of transferring the better class scholars to Reading schools, thus leaving in the Village a school which, under the circumstances, cannot be developed as the managers wish as only backward scholars would be left'.

The Chairman of the managers at this time was Sir Cyril Ashford after whom Ashford Avenue was named.

The Buildings

The school buildings needed to be enlarged again and in 1928 a new classroom was added and a *'hut for woodwork'* was erected at the end of the playground behind the toilets and sheds. Pupil capacity was now 200. In July 1930 a certificated teacher, Mr Cecil Simmons was appointed. The breakdown of pupil numbers was-

1st room – 60 children, 2 teachers
2nd room – 32 seniors, 1 teacher
3rd room – 76 children, 2 teachers
4th room – 35 infants, 1 teacher

Not all of the teachers were qualified – in those days it was quite usual for uncertificated staff to work alongside certificated teachers.

Even with this expansion the managers felt in February 1927 that there was no necessity for electricity to be connected to the school, though possibly to the headmaster's house but this would require a rise in his rent. Indoor sanitation to his house was agreed and his rent increased to £36 per annum. By 1932, the managers were asking when an electricity supply would be available to the school.

More new building completed in 1931 took capacity to 280 with 209 on roll. The new buildings faced on to the playground. In line with the Hadow report, Kidmore End School was reorganised as a junior school and in 1932 fifteen seniors from there transferred to Sonning Common.

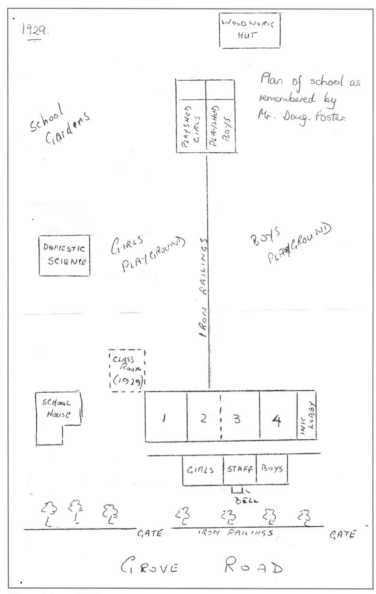

Plan of the school 1929

A breakdown of school costs for 1924/5 can be found in the manager's minutes and is as follows:

Total cost of the school	£1217. 16s 0d
Net cost to rates	£377. 13s 6d
Average attendance for the year 131 pupils	
Approx cost of each pupil to rates	£2 17s 6d

This is further expanded:

Salaries of teachers	£918 0s 0d	
Deduct three fifths	£551 2s 0d	
(paid by Board of Education grant)		£366 18.0d
Loan charges	£176 14s 8d	
Fuel and light	£23 8s. 3d	
Cleaner's wages and materials	£63 9s. 4d.	
Stationary/apparatus	£26 0s. 0d.	
Handwork material	£4 8s. 5d.	
Needlework material	£4 14s 10d.	
		£298 15s 6d
		£ 665 13s 6d
Deduct grant and substantive grant from		
Board of Education		£288 0s 0d
Approx cost to rates		£377 13s 6d

Compare this with the annual cost of the school today which is approximately £1,390,984.

The managers were very careful with school funds but agreed in February 1935 that if a wireless was paid for by voluntary contributions they were willing to pay the licence fee provided the wireless was used for *'teaching purposes'*.

Health

As well as the ever present problem of head lice, there were still regular epidemics of whooping cough, chicken pox, measles, German measles, scarlet fever and other diseases of childhood. These were not, perhaps helped by sanitary conditions at the school. An inclusion in the 1923 minutes is headed *'Absence of Sanitary Paper and Disinfectant'* and reads as follows:

> *'None is provided and pupils are obliged to use old pieces of newspaper in the W.Cs, a practice entirely objectionable and conducive to drain blockage.'*

The School Dentist visited infrequently and in 1936 dental defects were found in 172 children (64% of the total roll) and 109 accepted treatment.

The caretaker at this time was a Mr Middleton and his wife helped prepare and supervise at lunchtime. Most children were expected to go home for lunch and a letter to parents stated that those who did stay must remain on the premises for the entire period, those going home must not be allowed back on the premises until one o'clock. In 1931 there were on average 80 children having school dinner each day. Mr Forder strictly supervised those having dinner himself and was commended by the managers for the *'marked improvement in manners'* shown by pupils. There had been a problem with children coming and going because they had *'small shopping commissions to execute'* for their parents. The Local Education Authority further stated that they would have no responsibility for children not on the premises.

School dinners 1930

The 30 infant children were served with a bottle of hot milk daily in the winter months. This came from a local farmer named Saunders who pasteurised the milk at 160 degrees Fahrenheit for 20 minutes and sold it in one third of a pint bottles at a cost to children of ½ d a bottle. Two gallons of milk were supplied every day.

Punishment

Physical punishment (caning) was a very frequent occurrence for such misdemeanours as throwing apples in the playground, insolence, truancy, using a catapult in the playground and stealing money from billet (one of the evacuees). The number of strokes given varied between one and four depending on the seriousness of the 'crime'. Contrary to popular belief, perhaps, not all parents agreed with punishment to their children and former pupil John Earle recalls a mother coming onto the school premises and having a fight with Mr Forder over punishment meted out to her son.

One parent complained to the managers that Mr Forder had hit her son on the head – Mr Forder was called in to explain. The reason he gave was that the boy had an *'objectionable'* book. The managers wrote to the parent that the head's action was justified in the circumstances but asked Mr Forder to use authorised methods of punishment in future. The Education Committee recommended that punishments be carried out at the end of the school day. Mr Forder objected to this because marks might be left on pupils which could cause misunderstanding when the pupil returned home. It was agreed that he could defer punishment to the following morning.

Mrs Forder had a habit of wearing a silver thimble on her little finger and, as she went around the room would administer a sharp rap on the head if she spotted any mistakes in written work.

In February 1933, one forward looking manager, Mr Colombe, questioned physical punishment inflicted by the headmaster on girls. He was told that only one girl had been punished in this way (more than once according to the punishment book) during Mr Forder's tenure. Mr Colombe made clear that he was not suggesting there had been any abuse but was raising a general principle. It was agreed by the managers to abolish physical punishment for girls and infants. However, the Local Authority did not agree –

> *'The organisation section did not agree with the proposal of the managers that corporal punishment for infants and girls be abolished. They understand that it is very rare that it is inflicted but consider it desirable that it should be possible for head teachers where necessary, to inflict it.'*

No.	Name	Offence	Date of Offence	Punishment Awarded	Date of Punishment.	Rei
A16	Mr Gluning (Ealing)	Throwing apples in the	30.9.40	2 Strokes	30.9.40	JSJ
417	K Stevens	playground.		2 Strokes	30.9.40	JSJ
418	A. Smith (Ealing)	Insolence to Teacher.	22.10.40	2 Strokes	22.10.40	JSJ
419	A thelborne (Ealing)	Insolence to Teacher.	31.10.40	4 Strokes	31.10.40	JSJ
420	S. Bromley (Lee)	using Catapult in the playground	31.10.40	2 Strokes	31.10.40	JSJ.
421	J. Faulkner (Ealing)	Truancy.	14.11.40	2 Strokes	15.11.40	
422	h Miller Lee			1 Stroke		JSJ.
423	J McKay Lee			1 Stroke		
424	Som morgan.	Truancy.	2.12.40	2 Strokes	3.12.40	JSJ
425	Geo Hawes Lee.	misbehaviour at prayer Time	11.12.40	2 Strokes	11.12.40	

Extract from punishment book 1940 – 41

Sport

There is very little to be gleaned about school sport at this time although the managers congratulated Mr Forder when the school won the shields for all age groups in the Goring area sports.

It is worth noting that in 1945 a Mr and Mrs Grant presented a Sports Shield in memory of their son, Lieut. T. Grant (a former pupil) of the Gloucester regiment who was killed in action. The headteacher proposed that it be awarded to the boy who put up the best performance at the Annual Sports Meeting, to be decided by the judges on the day of the sports. The Shield was to be kept and displayed in the school. The Shield was presented for many years to the team that gave the best performance on Sports Day and can still be seen in the school. A trophy for the best sportsman was donated at a later date (Appendix 2) and it was a highlight of many pupils' school career to win it. It was agreed many years later that there should be a similar trophy for the best performance by a girl (Appendix 2).

Girls P.E. 1944

Boys P.E. 1944

Boys P.E. 1946/47 with Mr E. Martin

Staffing, inspections and reports

The school was regularly inspected by His Majesty's Inspectors (H.M.I.) and excellent reports were received by the school managers. Mr Forder disputed the Inspectors assertion that children should be classified by age, preferring to classify according to ability. The managers agreed with the headmaster:

> 'The question of the promotion of backward children was discussed and it was pointed out that there were no examinations for promotion but the Headteacher was endeavouring to arrange for every child to reach the top form for, at any rate, the last term of his school career.'

Mr Forder reported annually to the school managers on the staff and not always favourably. In 1934 Mr Hall was found to be unsatisfactory and it was agreed that he be persuaded to resign or his services dispensed with. By 1935 Mr Sandall had been appointed in his place. Mr Forder himself was congratulated for his efforts.

> 'Mr Forder has performed his duties to the entire satisfaction of the Managers. They also wish to congratulate him on the excellent report of H.M.I. and of his handling of his staff.'

Pupils received termly reports and a School Record card when they left the school. The School Record was an important document, presented in a manila envelope for safe keeping.

Oxfordshire Education Committee.

.... *Sonning Common C. Sch.* ....SCHOOL.

REPORT *for the*........*Summer*..................*term* 193 2

Name... *Beatrice Callis*. Class or Std...*VI*....

Times absent........*1*........ Times late.......*0*........
(Very Good, Good, Moderate, or Weak.)

English ... *V Good* .... Handwork ....

Geography... *Good* .... Gardening ....

History *Moderate* Cookery ....

Mathematics *V. Good* . Needlework *V Good* ....

Science .... *Good* ...... Drawing ....

Conduct...... *Good* .

General Remarks ... *Has worked very hard* . *and deserves her success.*

.... *C. Lucia Philp S Jordes* ...
Class Teacher.   Head Teacher.

Date ...*29 JUL 1932*...
5 SEP 1932

NEXT TERM BEGINS ON ....
10000/6/31.

I have examined the Report for the.......................Term.
Signature of Parent or Guardian

Beatrice Callis: termly report 1932

8. HEIGHT.
9. WEIGHT. } *Average physique*

10. VISION.   *Good.*

11. ATHLETIC DISTINCTIONS.

12. GENERAL REMARKS.
A quiet, well mannered, boy who tries hard with his work.

Philp S Jordes
Head Teacher.

Date *23 July 1945*.

Oxfordshire Education Committee.

SCHOOL RECORD.

Peter Pratt.

Peter Pratt : School Record 1945

World War 2

By 1938 measures were being put in place for the expected conflict to follow. It was agreed that A.R.P. (air raid precautions) and Special Constables meetings could be held in the school with no charge made except for heating, lighting and caretaker's remuneration. It was noted that the fitting of gas masks, gasproofing rooms and the provision of shelters were in the hands of local A.R.P. organisations and they would be responsible for any work or instructions involved. It was felt that children should remain in school under discipline rather than remain out of control outside although it was agreed that parents could withdraw their children in an emergency if they wished.

On 16th February a circular was received with details of these arrangements:

1. Schools not to be closed should war occur
2. Protection of children – headteacher to be nominated School Warden
3. No public Elementary School to be used for emergency purposes such as first-aid post or billeting
4. No teacher over 25 to volunteer for A.R.P. work or similar National Service which would interfere with their duties

Air-raid Shelters

The provision of shelters was discussed by the managers but it was decided that, at the present time, risk was low and no further action would be taken. However, stirrup pumps were provided by the Council.

> *'The desirability of digging trenches, providing sand-bag emplacements, sandbagging the windows up to a height of 5 foot or sending the children into the fields to refuge under hedges was discussed. It was agreed on account of the psychological effect on the children that it was desirable for them to continue normal school in the event of an air-raid.'*

Government Evacuation Scheme

In August 1939 the managers discussed arrangements for the expected influx of evacuees. It was agreed that it would be possible to accommodate twice as many children (600) if a shift system were employed. Use of Sonning Common Hall for infant children was also discussed. It had room for 105 on chairs and forms, a piano, a sink, 2 earth closets and electric light but no blinds.

By September 1939 the evacuees had arrived. There were 96 children from Westville Road School, Shepherd's Bush, 74 from Hanwell Bordesdon Road School, Ealing and 49 others. Their teachers came too and the shift system came into being, group 1 attending in the morning and group 2 in the afternoon.

(i) Boys shift plus Oxfordshire infants – 243 children under one headteacher, 11 men assistants, 1 woman assistant and 1 woodwork teacher
(ii) Girls shift and evacuee infants – 185 under 1 headteacher, and 8 women assistants

The Christmas holiday in 1939 was just 4 days, from 23rd December to 27th December with the school being open on either Christmas or Boxing Day with activities for the evacuees who must have felt the separation from their families much more keenly at this time.

The children from Westville Road School were fortunate – here is their school in February 1944:

Despite the war, education was to continue with as little disruption as possible. Circulars were received concerning double summer time school opening which was set at 9 o'clock and a threat of proceedings against any farmer or parent allowing school boys to be absent from school to take on farming work. Children were expected to bring their gas masks to school with them every day.

Form **At. 11.**

OXFORDSHIRE EDUCATION COMMITTEE.

_____

**Application for permission to take scholars to places of educational interest
under Article 44 (b) of the code for Elementary Schools.**

August 15 1913.

Name of School.	Date and time of proposed visit.	Number and standard (or class) of children.	Place or places to be visited.	Names of Teachers accompanying the scholars.
Eye & Dunsden Sonning Common Council School	Oct: 23 1913. (1.40 - 3.40)	Class I + II 15	Emmer Green Brick Works	Woodward. Frederick William
	March. 18. 1914 (10a.m - 12.a.m)	14	Huntley + Palmers Biscuit factory. Reading	
	March. 18. (1.40. - 3.40)	"	Forbury Gardens + Reading abbey Ruins	
	May. 20. 1914 (1.40 - 3.40)	14	Suttons Trial Grounds Reading	
	July. 15. 1914. (1.40-3.40)	15	Reading Museum	

Object of the Visit :

1. To give the children some idea of the manufactures + industries carried on in the district

2. By visiting Museum + ruins to help them to get a better idea of history.

J.W.Woodward. Head Teacher.

Approved on behalf of the Education Committee.

F.Elford
26/8/13
Education Secretary.

Approved on behalf of the Board of Education.

Application for permission to take pupils on a trip - 1913

World war 2 child's gas mask

Wartime had an effect on the academic standard of the school. In 1941 Mr Forder reported to the managers that he felt standards were about one year behind for a number of reasons including frequent changes of staff, disorganisation and low standard of attainment and discipline among evacuee children, particularly those aged 11 plus. Inefficiency of teaching staff was put down to wartime fatigue.

Some teachers were struggling and staff absence was high. Mrs Jones suffered from a nervous complaint of some kind and in 1943 was frequently absent and not really able to cope with her job when she was there:

> 'it is frequently as much as she can do to drag herself into school by 9.00 a.m. and when she does arrive, can only sit at her table and work in spasms and often she cannot last out the day'.

Mr Lockwood (Pop) had problems of a different nature. Mr Forder reported:

> 'The standard of work and conduct accepted by Mr Lockwood is appallingly low. It is only necessary to glance at the state of the classroom, desks and textbooks to know what the exercise books and note books are going to be like.'

Mrs Smith and Miss Quick are described as the best two teachers in the school, doing really good work.

Casualties of War

In November 1944, Mr Forder gave this list of former scholars who had given their lives in the war.

Flight Sergt Philip Swan R.A.F

Flight Sergt Kenneth Goddard R.A.F

Flight Sergt Derrick Nichol R.A.F

Corpl Dennis Wylde 17/21 Lancers

Seaman Frederick Lanning R.N.

L/Sergt Cyril Clayton Hants Regt

(apologies if this is an incomplete list)

F/Sgt E.O. Bule R.A.F

Sgt A.E. Edwards R.A.F

Stoker C.L. Gale R.N.

Lieut T.D. Grant Gloster Rgt

Pte S. Pryke Ox and Bucks L.I.

Able Seaman Frederick Tolhurst R.N.

Mr Forder requested that before he retired he should be allowed to present a plaque to hang in the school which would preserve the memory of the old scholars who lost their lives in the war. You can still see the plaque today with another name added from a later conflict (more of this in a later chapter).

Raising of the school leaving age

In 1947 the school leaving age was to be raised to 15 which meant further accommodation problems for the school. In late 1946 the Ministry of Works approved a scheme to build two detached huts to consist of a kitchen and dining room, a classroom and woodwork room. Buildings such as this were being erected all over the country and were known as HORSAs (Hutting Operation for the Raising of the School leaving Age). The classroom HORSA stood on the playground and was in use until it was demolished to make way for the new Bishopswood School building in 2000. The other HORSA, used variously over the years as a dining hall, classroom, art room and resource centre made way for the new Year 6 building in 2003.

HORSA building 1990s

Notable events during the Headship of Mr Forder

Some teachers whose names were to have a later impact on the school commenced duties during this time. Mr E. M. Martin was appointed on August 29th 1939 although he soon left to join the RAF. It was recorded in October 1945 that Sgt Martin hoped to be demobilised under Scheme B and to return to the school. An uncertificated teacher, Miss Nesta Evans joined the staff in 1944 along with a Miss Callis. Miss Evans was on the staff until 1977 but by then she had taken courses to become a qualified teacher and had achieved promotion to Head of the Infant department. Also, in 1946 the first Parent Teacher Association was formed.

In 1947 Mr Forder informed the managers that he would retire from his post and Mr A. G. Miller of Hook Norton was appointed to take the Headteacher's role from 1st November.

Chapter Four

A Pupil's story - John Earle

A Sunday School trip (chapel in Blounts Court Road) circa 1937.
John is third from the right.

John Earle was born in June 1927 and has lived most of his life in Sonning Common, apart from a brief period when his family moved to Reading after the death of his mother. He attended Sonning Common Council School from 1931 until August 1941 when he left school at the age of 14 years.

John has fond memories of some teachers but recalls that most of the time he hated school and could not wait to leave. Mr Forder – known as Gaffer – was the headteacher. Miss Cobb was his first teacher in the infants. The classroom was at the end of what we now call the long corridor – the classrooms housed children of increasing age until they moved to the top classes where the library is now.

John moved on to Mrs Clayton's class – 'Fatty Clayton' – as she was known. He does not remember this class happily as it was during this time that his mother died when he was just 5 years old. He had to sit by a girl in class (not through choice) and was telling her that his mother had died the night before when the teacher slapped him round the head for talking in class. His friends included John Haddington, Peter and David Vivian, Bill Wells, Reggie White and Bob Peat.

Moving along the corridor, the next part was a section with sinks for handwashing – the toilets were outside at the end of the playground where there was also some cover for pupils to shelter at playtime when the weather was inclement. These toilets remained in use into the 1980s and the playsheds are now storage areas and tabletennis playing areas. There were two stoke holes at either end of the school, where the coal was stored which heated classroom radiators.

John moved on to Miss Hoare's class and then to Mrs Smith, Miss Saunders and Mr Sandall. The top corridor housed Mr Forder's, Mrs Smith's and Mr Lockwood's classes.

Term 1, 1937 Mrs Smith

Term 3 1938, Mrs Smith's class

Evacuees

John remembers when his family had evacuees staying with them and, of course, attending the school. Names such as Gluning (known as Sticky Gluning) and the Page twins from Ealing have remained in his memory. Other evacuees came from Shepherd's Bush and Wales. The evacuees' teachers came too – Pruno, Armstrong, Topping and Richenson were teachers John recalls. The school was so overcrowded at this time that pupils attended for half day shifts only, one week mornings, one week afternoons. The report below from Autumn 1938 shows that John was to attend in the afternoon from 1.20 to 3.35.

Autumn 1938 Mr Sandall

John recalls many physical punishments during his school years – (striking children or throwing things at them appears to have been a casual everyday occurrence). John, however, made it to the formal punishment book just once when on October 4th 1938 (aged 11 years) he was given 2 strokes of the cane for 'disobedience'. This probably resulted from an occasion when the boys lined up too slowly after breaktime and Gaffer went along the row of boys giving each a clip round the ear. John and Gareth Evans 'ducked' and were told 'you'll get yours later'. Looks as though they did!

No.	Name	Offence	Date of Offence	Punishment Awarded	Date of Punishment.
325	Walter Marshall.	Misbehaviour in	25.10.37	2 Strokes	25.10.37
326.	Douglas Goodwin.	Passage.		2 Strokes	25.10.37.
327.	Robt Hoadley.	Bad behaviour in classroom during teacher's absence.	9.11.37.	2. Strokes	9.11.37.
328	Walter Marshall.	Disobedience	15.11.37	3 Strokes	15.11.37
329	Keneth Gale.	Bullying a small boy on way home from school	26.11.37	2 Strokes.	26.11.37.
1938					
330	Douglas Goodwin.	Misbehaviour Class	4.2.38	2 Strokes.	4.2.38
331	Fred Kew.	Throwing stones in Playground	8.2.38	2 Strokes	8.2.38
332	Kenneth Gale.	} Bullying	6.5.38	2 Strokes	6.5.38
333	Peter White	}		2 Stroke	6.5.38.
34	Johnson Noman	Laziness & Misbehaviour	11.7.38	2 Strokes	11.7.38.
45	John Earle.	Disobedience	4.10.38	2 Strokes	4.10.38
46	Alec Evans		4.10.38	" "	4.10.38.
41	Cyril Austin	} Filthy Behaviour	7.11.38	Two Strokes	8.11.38.
48.	Philip Morning	} outside School gate.	7.11.38		

4ᵗʰ October 1938

Spring 1939 Miss Saunders

Summer 1939 Miss Saunders

CHAPTER 4: A PUPIL'S STORY - JOHN EARLE

Gardening, P.E. and woodwork were taught by specialist teachers. John recalls that he had two sets of footwear, boots for school and shoes for Sunday. One day, during a P.E. lesson he jumped and accidentally landed on the teacher, Miss Denton's, foot with his heavy boots. The woodwork teacher was Mr. Naish who taught in a room shared by other schools. There was oil lighting and a treadle lathe. John was instructed in gardening and, from age 13, each pair of boys had their own small plot of garden. Other subjects were taught by the class teacher – sex education was not part of the curriculum!

In order to move on to Henley Grammar School, examinations had to be taken and passed. John's father told him he could not afford for him to stay at school but this delighted John.

John could not wait to leave school which he did in the summer of 1941, aged 14. He started work at Vincent's (cars) in Reading earning the sum of 3½ d an hour.

Leaving school report 15th August 1941

Chapter Five
Mr A. G. Miller (1947 – 1956)

The next ten years saw an increase in numbers of pupils on roll and the move towards opening a new secondary school for South Oxfordshire – Chiltern Edge School which opened its doors in September 1957. In 1952 Sonning Common became a parish in its own right, separate from Eye and Dunsden and in May 1953 the school changed its name to Sonning Common County School in preparation for the day when it would no longer be an all age school but a primary school (age 4-11) only.

Mr Arthur Miller took up his duties on 1st November 1947 with 270 pupils on roll rising to 295 by March the following year and 327 by 1949. In May of that year the managers noted that pressure on accommodation was becoming a problem with 338 children on roll partly due to *'squatters in Kingswood Camp'*.

In 1955 the 330 pupils were organised as follows:

Infants II	35
Infants I	<u>35</u>
	<u>70</u>
Juniors I	38
Juniors II	35
Juniors III	33
Juniors IV	<u>36</u>
	<u>142</u>
Seniors 2	36
Seniors 3	31
Seniors 4	27
Seniors 5	<u>24</u>
	<u>118</u>
Total number of pupils	**<u>330</u>**

It was clear at this time that the removal of all senior pupils in 1957 would impact the school in many ways and it provided the L.E.A. with the perfect excuse not to spend much money on improvements, especially for pupil accommodation as it would not be needed for very long. One class had to be accomodated in the Congregational Hall as there was not enough space on the main site and the headteacher's house was already being used for small group work.

A. Miller (Headmaster)

Mr Miller and class 1949

There was considerable stability in staffing during these years. Amongst these were Miss Cordwell (who married to become Mrs Coombs), Mr Ewart Martin who became head of Rotherfield Secondary School and then Chiltern Edge School's first headteacher, Miss Watson (who married to become Mrs Lunn), Mr Hutchence, Mr Judd, Mrs Clayton, Mr Lockwood and Mr Higgins. Joining the staff in June 1950 was Mr A. Enever who would become the next head for a short period between 1956 and 1957. The headteacher's wife, Mrs Miller taught needlework on several afternoons each week.

Mr Higgins and class 1949

Back row: Wendy Beeton, ?, Janet Barry, Audrey Farr, Jill Mount, Ann Phillips, Jenny Ritchens?, Veronica?, Charlotte Lear, Zena Ball,
2nd row: Avril Wilson, Judy Green, Michael Kernick, Tony Summerfield, John Richardson, Jim Chandler, ? Phillips, Don Taylor, Peter Stark, ?.?, Raymond Knee, Marion Thorn, ?
3rd row: Sheila Roberts, ?, Ruth Cox, Mr Higgins, Pam Norris, Pauline Luckett, Susan Nash (Bean)
Front row: Stuart Stacey, ?, Christopher Burling, Brian White, Lennard Pearce, Martin Evans

Mrs Lunn and class 1949. Miss Watson became Mrs Lunn in 1955 so if the date is correct this is Miss Watson.

Mr Lockwood and class 1949

Miss Cordwell and cookery class 1949

School Uniform

In 1948 Mr Miller told the managers that he would gradually like to introduce an optional school uniform consisting a cap and blazer for boys, beret and gymslip for girls. It was agreed that these should be in blue and with a school badge. As you can see below, not everyone wore it.

1952 -53 Martyn Evans supplied this photo. He is 5th from the right in the back row. The teacher is Miss Dover.

Sport

Sport continued to be a very important and successful aspect of school life as it still is today.

1949 was a particularly successful year. The school was runner up to Henley Grammar School in the South Oxon Senior Shield and 10 Sonning Common children won places in the County Sports. Four pupils won County Championships:

High Jump Group 1: 1st John Peachy, 2nd Anthony Prior

High Jump group 2: 1st Peter Drayton

All 3 boys beat previous county records

Long Jump Group 1: Edith Ockwell

75 yards Group 3: Cynthia Smith

John Peachy went on to represent Oxfordshire at High jump in the All-England Sports and Edith Ockwell in the 100 yards.

Trevor Sheppard captained the South Oxfordshire schools football XI, John Stone and Charles Sparkes were also selected to play. The netball team won every game they played in the Henley and District League.

Mr Martin – boys sports 1949?

Mr Martin and Mr Miller with boys' football team 1948/49

Mr Enever and the 1951 football team

1951 netball team

Here is Ken Evans winning at Sports Day – still wearing his school tie! Most noticeable is the total lack of buildings in the background.

Premises

As early as 1948 there was discussion of the need for a new building for the infant children. This did not happen until the 1960s. In the meantime, the old woodwork room was adapted to become the infant room by the addition of a square of linoleum.

A 1950 report from His Majesty's Inspectors recommended improvements to the facilities, especially for the staff. There was only one staff lavatory which was shared by all staff and approached through the boys 'offices' and no separate washing facility for staff. The report suggested that a washing facility and w.c. for women staff was essential, as was a washbasin for men. The senior girls were to be provided with lockers if funds allowed and storage space, which was difficult to find, must be secured for the storage of P.T. and science equipment. In the event, shelves and sliding doors were placed under work benches.

The staffroom was big enough for only two thirds of the staff to occupy at one time and did not have proper chairs. There were improvements by 1952 and a recommendation from Captain Pullein-Thompson (chairman of managers) that:

> 'a small lazy chair be provided as a necessity for the staffroom'.

Some of the premises improvement such as making seats to go in a 'chimney piece' would be undertaken by senior pupils. Additional ground was required for the gardening classes too. In 1951 it was decided to improve the external appearance of the school by enclosing the front flowerbeds in a one foot high wall to retain the soil and prevent damage by animals. The cost would not exceed £5 if the senior boys did the work as a Spring project and second hand materials were used. After 1957 it would no longer be possible to employ this free labour force as all pupils would transfer to other schools at age eleven.

Health and Safety

Huge outbreaks of disease which closed the school are no longer reported but in 1953 one child contracted tuberculosis meningitis requiring a mass radiography unit to visit the school. Ninety nine per cent of parents agreed that their children be x-rayed. Outbreaks of common childhood diseases such as measles were still occurring regularly and, at times, only 80% of the children were present.

Problems with the traffic in Grove Road continued and in 1951 the headeacher reported on the danger caused by school buses passing each other outside the school. It was decided to insist that all buses must approach the school from the same direction. It was also decided to recommend to the Highways Committee that they kerb the pathway outside the school as a safety measure but they declined to do this.

Curriculum

Visits from the Inspectors (H.M.I.) were a regular occurrence and following a 1950 visit Mr Miller was asked to inform his staff of the highly satisfactory nature of the report. The Inspector was particularly impressed by the Puppetry Club and he made a film strip of their activities, a copy of which was presented to the school.

Some examples of pupils work have survived the years and, in many respects there is not a huge amount of change although today's children would struggle with £.s.d.

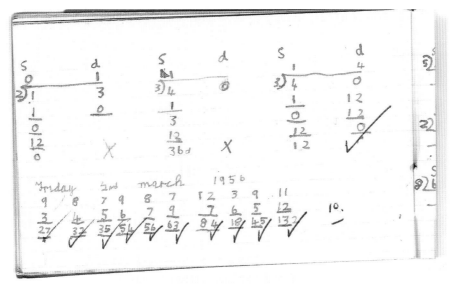

Douglas Pound's arithmetic 1956 (aged 7)

Here is Douglas Pound with his class in 1955 when he was 7 years old in J1 (first year junior).

Back row: Jennifer King, Leslie King, ?, David Silcox, ?, Richard Whitehouse, Heather Brown, ?, Valerie Gunston
Middle row: Andrew Cook, Douglas Pound, Margaret Osers, ?, Lynne Hoadley, Marion Fowler, Lesley James, ??, ?,
Front row: Andrew Silver, ? Talbot, Barry Webb, Gordon Stansbury, Michael Skidmore, ?, Martin Tubb, ?, Johnnie Haines?

steps
Flag
Tree
roses
Pram
Canapy
basket
Age
pat
brom
door
mary-golds
cortops
window
gras
oasis
Ring
baboy
tras

This spelling test from a similar time is not much different to one we could see today – and the mistakes are the same too!

OXFORDSHIRE EDUCATION COMMITTEE
SONNING COMMON COUNTY SCHOOL

SCHOOL REPORT

Name D. Pound   Form Class I   Term II   1955
Number in Form 38   Position 3   Times absent   Times late

	TERM'S WORK	EXAMINATION Marks	EXAMINATION Position	REMARKS
English Oral				
English Written	B	49		V. good.
		45	4	
Mathematics	A	100	1	Excellent №2
Social Studies Geog.	B	50		
Social Studies Hist.		50		
Science or Nature Study	B	50		
Art & Craft	C	75		
Domestic Science, Woodwork and Metalwork				
Needlework Gardening				
P.E. & Games				

A Very Good   B Good   C Average   D Below Average   E Not Satisfactory

Most Satisfactory.

D. Fisher   Form Master/Mistress

An excellent beginning.
Next term begins   AGMiller   Headmaster

Douglas Pound school report 1955

OXFORDSHIRE EDUCATION COMMITTEE
SONNING COMMON COUNTY SCHOOL

SCHOOL REPORT

Name **Bridgeman. Dorean.** Form **3** Term **Spring** 195 **3**
Number in Form **28** Position **1ˢᵗ** Times absent **2** Times late

		TERM'S WORK	EXAMINATION Marks	EXAMINATION Position	REMARKS
English	Oral	B	121/150	6/23	Good work has been done throughout the term F.W.P.
	Written	B+			
Mathematics		b	96/100	2/23	Has worked well and shown interest. F.W.P.
Social Studies	Geog.	B-			Good. works well. F.W.P.
	Hist.	B			Very good work. E.H.E.
Science or Nature Study		S.			Good.
Art & Craft		B			Capable, but must adopt a more serious approach to this work
Domestic Science, Woodwork and Metalwork		S			Works with intelligence
Needlework Gardening		B.			Good
P.E. & Games		B+			Is keen on games and P.T. and has done good work

A Very Good   B Good   C Average   D Below Average   E Not Satisfactory

Doreen has worked well this term, and has shown marked progress. She is a helpful and reliable child in class.

Form ~~Master~~/Mistress

An excellent result.

Next term begins **13th April 1953.** Headmaster

I have examined the Report for the
Signature of Parent or Guardian
This slip should be torn off and re

Doreen Bridgeman's school report 1953

Doreen throwing the javelin 1954
(Brenda Barwell in the background)

Punishment

Caning continued to be permitted but judging by the entries in the book, Mr Miller had less appetite for it with this one page covering six years. However, a marked increase in incidences of smoking – perhaps cigarettes became more available after the war years and the pupils were older, aged up to 15 years.

No.	Name	Offence	Date of Offence	Punishment Awarded	Date of Punishment.	Remarks
686	Williams G.	Insolence & slackness	13.2.51	1 stroke	13.3.51	This boy proved very difficult
687	Brennan Dennis.	Insolence to two class teachers	6-6-51 7-6-51	2 strokes on hand	11-2-51	Gamul attitude very
688	Parker Geoffrey	Destroying toilet paper in lavatory	9-9-52 2.40pm	—	9-9-52	For revenge ... plus detention.
689	Parker Geoffrey	do.	9-9-52. 3-45pm	—	11-9-52	
690	New Harold	Truanting & smoking in lavatory	14-11-52	—	19-11-52	After warning
691	Willis Brian	Smoking in lavatory	14-11-52	—	19-11-52	
692	Alan Tull	Insolence to teacher on field	3-12-74	2 — —	3-12-54	After field had ...
693	Raymond Knee	One weeks truancy	14-21-3-55	2 -- - --	22-3-55	
694	Terence Tull	Destroying toilet paper in lavatory	3-X-55	2 strokes on seat	3-X-55	These boys are ... terrorising other ...
695	Bogus Wheelock	..	3-X-55	-- - -	3-X-55	
696	Boswell Anthony	Truancy	8-X-55	2 strokes on hand	6-X-55	Fifth form boys — several days.
697	Hornby Malcolm.	..	8-X-55	-	6-X-55	
698	J. Thompson	Smoking in lunch hour	28.6.56	2 strokes on hand	28.6.56	
699	R. Taylor	..	28.6.56	..	28.6.56	
700	G Norris	Throwing stones at boys in bus	22.11.56	2 strokes on hand	23.11.56	This boy was warned bad behaviour ...
701	V. Grubble	Insolence to Mrs Bullough (written)	18.3.57	1 stroke on hand	18.3.57	
702	R. Gregory	Smoking	18.3.57	1 stroke on hand	18.3.57	
703	G. Norris	Smoking.	18.3.57			

Department. Sonning Common C.E. Sen. School. ... A.G. Miller ... Principal Teac

Extract from punishment book

Opening of Chiltern Edge School

The Haddow report of 1926 paved the way for the educational separation of children at age 11 years by substituting 'primary' for 'elementary' and introducing 'secondary' for all post-primary age pupils. There would be two secondary groups; grammar and modern. Thus a need was established for a secondary modern school in Sonning Common although this would not actually be opened until 1957.

There was already a secondary school in Rotherfield but Sonning Common pupils were not in its catchment area.

The catchment areas were clearly laid down so if, for example, a child lived in Peppard, he was designated Rotherfield School and not South Oxon Secondary Modern (Chiltern Edge).

Rotherfield Secondary Modern	South Oxon Secondary Modern
Grey's Green	Sonning Common
Highmoor	Kidmore End
Peppard	Mapledurham
Stoke Row	Micklands
Nettlebed	Dunsden
Nuffield	

By October 1953 a site had been selected for the new school, the landowner was willing to sell the land and negotiations were progressing. In May 1954 the Education committee approved the sketch plans. The first instalment of the school was estimated at £100,000. In February 1955 tenders were invited for the new school and work was in hand by October 1955.

Mr Miller resigned in 1956 to take up an appointment as head of a secondary school in Somerset and the school managers recorded their appreciation of the *very great services* he had given to the school. It was decided by the managers to appoint Mr A Enever as acting headteacher and to advertise the permanent headship of the new secondary modern school at the same time as the primary headship. It was intended that the secondary school would open in September 1956 but it was not until September 1957 that Chiltern Edge School was finally opened with its first headteacher, Mr Ewart Martin.

Chapter Six
Mr A. Enever (1956 – 1957)

Although Mr Alex Enever was acting headteacher for only a short time his headship marked the end of Sonning Common as an all age school and heralded the opening of what the next head, Mr Johnson, called a new school.

For the final term in May 1957 the school numbers were as follows:

Seniors	Form V	14 pupils
	Form 1V	24 pupils
	Form 111	37 pupils
	Form 11	33 pupils
Juniors	Class 4	34 pupils
	Class 3	38 pupils
	Class 2	40 pupils
	Class 1	32 pupils
Infants	1	29 pupils
	11	29 pupils
	111	28 pupils

Mr A. Enever

The total roll was 338 pupils.

From the above numbers we can see that although we are always told that numbers of children in each class was huge, it was not, in fact, necessarily the case. The removal of the senior section (108 pupils) was going to make a big difference to school numbers, create much needed space and, effectively, make a different school entirely.

June Huggins
(Fisher)'s class 1957

Back row: Laurence Austin, John Bains, Jim Enever,?, Brian Pope, ?, Martyn Tubb, David Knight
Next part row: Howard Andrews, Barry Fisher, ?, Clive Clayton, Christopher Dove, ?, Sonia Bowles
Middle row: Rosemary Trott, Elizabeth Hutchins(?), Vivien Ellis, Heather Brown, Susan Kernick(?), Jimmy Skidmore, Graham Keil, Robert Landsley, Lawrence Wilson (?), ?, Carole Smith, Diane Woods
Front row: June Huggins, Kate Soden, Valerie Parsons, ?, Ann Audoire, Barry Webb, Teresa Radziun, Susan Harris, Gerda Van Well

Martyn Tubb (back row) is alleged to have had this exchange with his teacher Mrs Fisher, who was about to rap his knuckles:

'Don't hit my knuckles today, do it tomorrow'

'Why tomorrow?'

'Because I'm not coming tomorrow!'

Premises

Mr Enever recommended immediate changes to the buildings including the adaptation of the HORSA block to provide two infant classrooms with their own washing and sanitary accommodation, a new sanitary block for the juniors (estimated cost £1100), enlargement of classes 1 and 2 to provide a hall (estimated cost £1500) and the creation of a third infant classroom on the site of the playshed (estimated cost £4000). However, the Education Committee decided that as a new headteacher had already been appointed it would be better to wait until he was in post in case he had different ideas.

The school managers were not happy about this, especially with regard to sanitary arrangements. Attention was drawn to the unsatisfactory state and structure of the boys' lavatories for 150 boys. Among other faults:

(i)   moisture seeps through the wall into the playground
(ii) there is only one combined entrance and exit measuring three feet or so wide
(iii) there is less than ten feet of effective length of urinal
(iv) inadequacy of the W.C.s

School managers have always had to focus on 'sanitary' arrangements (see comments from 1923). Beware prospective school governors if you are invited to join the Environment Committee.

Curriculum

Mr Enever decided that major changes to the curriculum and the way in which pupil progress was reported should be left for the new headteacher.

OXFORDSHIRE EDUCATION COMMITTEE
SONNING COMMON COUNTY SCHOOL

SCHOOL REPORT

Name _June Huggins_   Form _J2_   Term _3_   195_7_
Number in Form _38_   Position ____   Times absent ____   Times late ____

		TERM'S WORK	EXAMINATION Marks	Position	REMARKS
English	Oral Reading	E	28% /30	12	Written work very good.
	Written	B	115 /20	13	
Mathematics		C	58 /100	19	Fairly good, but needs to work hard.
Social Studies	Geog. Hist.		39 /50	20	
Science or Nature Study			22 /25	12	
Art & Craft		C			
Domestic Science, Woodwork and Metalwork					
Needlework Gardening		C			
P.E. & Games		C			

A Very Good   B Good   C Average   D Below Average   E Not Satisfactory

June takes great pride in her work & is always meticulously neat and careful.

M. Passingham   Form Master/Mistress

Next term begins _4 SEP 1957_   A. Enever, Headmaster

June Huggins school report 1957

School trips continued to take place including to the British Museum and the Natural History Museum for older pupils. The Seniors were even offered a choice of lesson for one hour on Fridays. The choice was between aero modelling, light craft, school magazine club, painting in oils, French and cookery for boys. Golden Time in the 50s!

One innovation was that the Parent Teacher Association was invited to place one of its members on the Managing Body.

On 5th April 1957 Mr R B Johnson, presently deputy head of Sawston Primary School, Cambridge was offered the permanent headship; he asked for time to consider and this was granted. Following a short delay he accepted the post and became the fourth permanent headteacher of the school and the first of Sonning Common County Primary School.

Chapter Seven
Mr R. B. Johnson (1957 – 1977)

Mr R B Johnson (known as Johnny by staff and pupils) took the reins in September 1957 and opened the new Sonning Common County Primary School. At age 11 years pupils would now move on to Henley Grammar School if they passed the eleven plus examination or Chiltern Edge Secondary Modern School which opened at the same time.

Mr R. B. Johnson

This arrangement ended in September 1965 when the last group of pupils faced selection by the 11+. Children born after the beginning of September 1954 transferred into the new comprehensive system, the vast majority from Sonning Common moving to Chiltern Edge School.

This period saw huge changes in the population of Sonning Common. Houses were built around Kennylands Road, Blounts Court Road, Brind's Corner, Red House Drive and Baskerville Road and with these developments came lots and lots and lots of children. In 1966 Mr Johnson estimated that 350 new houses had been, or would be, built in the catchment area but the school managers felt this to be an underestimate. The school roll grew from 281 pupils in summer 1958 to 682 in summer 1974.

Year (summer term)	Number on roll
1958	281 (26 from Checkendon Hostel)
1959	282 (36 from Checkendon Hostel)
1960	270 (31 from Checkendon Hostel)
1961	266
1962	286
1963	282
1964	301 (33 from Peppard)
1965	377 (33 from Peppard, 23 from Emmer Green which was in Oxfordshire at this time)
1966	412 (32 from Peppard, 31 from Emmer Green)
1967	481 (44 from Peppard, 53 from Emmer Green)
1968	573 (47 from Peppard, 63 from Emmer Green)
1969	627 (56 from Peppard, 73 from Emmer Green)
1970	649 (53 from Peppard, 87 from Emmer Green)
1971	650 (59 from Emmer Green)
1972	672 (63 from Emmer Green)
1973	666 (68 from Emmer Green)
1974	682 (64 from Emmer Green) Numbers would have exceeded 700 had admission of Rising 5s not been refused.
1975	643
1976	

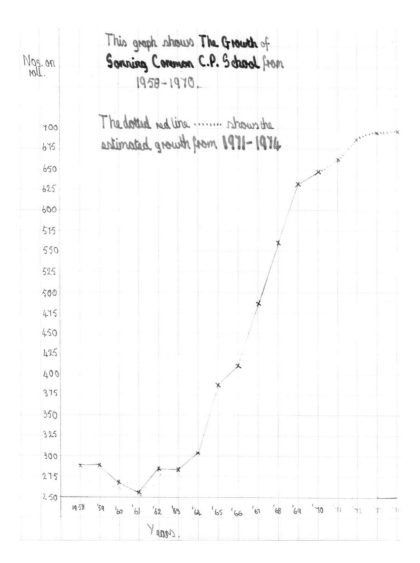

This graph, by an unnamed pupil, shows the growth of the school between 1958 and 1970 and the estimated growth in the years following – not a bad estimate at all. The new school opened on 4th September with 246 children, 8 teachers and a Headmaster. Teaching staff for the infants were Mrs Cook and Mrs Clayton and for the juniors, Mrs Fisher, Miss Passingham, Miss Evans, Mr Higgins (Deputy Headmaster), Mrs Enever and Mr Lockwood who taught 'backward' children in this streamed arrangement.

The school was now able to have a hall which was used for assembly, music, indoor P.E., art, dancing and small group work whilst part of it was the school library.

Numbers grew and grew and in 1971 it was being suggested that a second primary school should be built in Sonning Common to take 200 children. In October 1971 Mr Johnson reported to his managers, as fact, that a new school was to be built and would be ready in 1975. By April 1975 the idea had been dropped, initially because of planning difficulties and lack of funds but it was beginning to be understood that numbers on roll were going to stabilise and fall in the coming years.

Checkendon Hostel

The Checkendon Hostel housed displaced Polish refugee families. It was felt that when the school changed to primary age only there would be more places available which could be filled by children from the Hostel. Schools nearer to the Hostel were mainly 2 teacher schools and could be *'swamped'* by large influxes of additional pupils. In 1958, 26 children from the Hostel were bussed into school each day. This number increased to 36 in 1959. Although Mr Johnson welcomed the children and visited the camp to watch Polish dancing he had this to say to the Managers in April 1959:

> *'I suggest a generous staffing ratio should be allowed because of the absorption of a high proportion of alien children. These children, with their language barrier, create particular teaching problems, and because of their background and environment create many social problems. It is only due to the work of a competent staff of teachers, all of whom are good disciplinarians, that these displaced alien children, some of whom suffer from an appallingly low social background, have been accommodated in our school without detrimental effects upon our own English children. After two years of successfully absorbing this proportion of children from mixed European families with their Hostel background, national and family hatreds, and in some cases a marked dislike of the English, it is fair to make these statements and time they were made.'*

The Polish children had left the school, mostly being re-housed in other areas by January 1961 and Mr Johnson was proud to report that 3 children from homes speaking only Polish had gained places at grammar school. He also reported that in three and a half years he did not receive one complaint from any parent of the Polish children but many thanks and messages of appreciation.

Premises

The increasing numbers on roll made premises development a priority during the Johnson years. Improvements to the HORSA block (where the Bishopswood School building now stands) were made to make it suitable for younger children. Patio doors were installed, opening onto the field, sinks and new flooring were added - these rooms had previously housed the woodwork and craft room. 1960 saw the first indoor toilets for pupils.

Mr Johnson foresaw the huge increase in the size of the school during the 1960s and toured the village to see for himself some of the building projects which were springing up. He even went so far as to pretend to be a prospective buyer so that he could obtain information about the size and scale of new developments. He warned his managers and through them the County Council that the school would have to be extended but his warnings were not acted on very quickly. When he first suggested the purchase of 1 1/2 acres on the Lea Road side of the school in 1957/58 the land was priced as agricultural land at £250 per acre but by the time the County Council completed the purchase in 1964, they were in competition with developers and paid £5000 per acre. In 1961 he renewed his request for a new hall to be built so that the temporary hall (now library) could be used as 2 classrooms. This was agreed by full County Council and reported in local newspapers but then axed by the Minister of Education as an economy measure in 1963.

In September 1964, 299 children were on roll but this was expected to rise by 100 towards the end of the school year as 125 new houses were expected to be occupied by then and a further 180 the following year. Children from areas of Emmer Green (parts of which were in Oxfordshire) were also in the catchment area and Reading Council had said they would not be accepted in Reading schools. Caversham Park Primary School did not open until 1970. To cope with the rising numbers of pupils, additional teaching staff were recruited. Mr Derek Carter replaced Mr Wilson in 1963 and became Deputy Headteacher on the retirement of Mr Higgins and in April 1965 Mr Stuart Pitson joined the staff.

By September 1965 all available space including the library, school hall, parts of the school house and the canteen was being used for teaching. Morning assemblies and public functions took place in the corridors. Mr Johnson stood on a box at one end and all the children squashed in (everyone had to stand for the entire assembly). Mr Johnson was looking at accommodation away from the main buildings, notably St Michael's Hall, behind the Catholic Church which became a junior classroom for 40+ nine to ten year olds in May 1966 with Mr Pitson as their teacher. The children had to walk down to their classroom, back for lunch and down again for afternoon lessons. Their playground was where the church car park is now. Mr Pitson recalls two old gentlemen who would come every Tuesday and Thursday to watch his class having a P.E. lesson and Matthew Wickens, a pupil in that class, would walk about on his hands to impress them. Here is Mr Pitson's class in 1967 with Matthew Wickens standing on the left in the middle row.

By 1967, plans were underway for a new infant department and two temporary Elliott classrooms on the edge of the small playground relieved pressure slightly. In May, work on the new buildings began and was expected to be completed and the buildings ready for occupation in the summer term 1968. Despite the fact that it was not ready on time, the children and teachers moved in on 2nd May 1968. Mr Johnson wrote to his managers:

'On Tuesday 30th April I re-opened school and admitted 512 children. I began equipping and preparing the new Infant department immediately as though it was ready, ignoring all protests, expressed doubts and unco-operative acts. I engaged a volunteer force of members of staff and mothers to try and clean the place. On Thursday, 2nd May, I moved 200 infants into the new department. Many could not get into their classrooms and spent the day in the cloakrooms. Not one classroom was finished; the hall floor had not been finished, nor was it usable. On 3rd

May I ordered all workmen out of the classrooms. On 6th May, 38 new infants were admitted and a further 25 on Tuesday 7th May, into conditions that were chaotic.'

There were concerns that children would be distracted from their work by low windows which were quite close to houses on the Lea Road side. It was agreed to plant tall hedges along the boundary but it was not agreed to cover the lower part of all windows in the new building. In the summer term of 1969 the six infant classes were already overstretched with, 40, 40, 41, 46, 47, 46 in each room and another class in the infant hall.

The exterior of the junior building was painted during term time and this did cause some distraction. Mr Johnson wrote in the log book:

'One of the painters happened to be an out of work conjuror/juggler who could balance tins of paint, small ladders, brooms, paint brushes etc., etc., in the most unlikely positions at improbable angles, which he regularly did for the enjoyment of the children. In addition, he had a repertoire of modern songs and frequently practised his party piece which was an excellent sound picture of an express train speeding through the classrooms, school hall and corridors.'

Health and Safety

Fire drill has always been held in schools and Mr Johnson was keen to keep everyone up to the mark. On one famous occasion he lay on the floor of his office during a fire drill, waiting for someone to realise he was missing and 'rescue' him. No-one did.

He also tried to have fire doors put into all classrooms as the only escape for some pupils in the event of a real fire would have been through the windows. In the 1980s, the radical suggestion that everyone should have a practical escape route was <u>still</u> waiting to be implemented.

Whenever we think times have changed we find that, in many respects, they have not. In 1957 Mr Johnson raised concerns about the safety of children leaving school. In those days there were school buses taking children to Emmer Green and Checkendon and pupils were apt to cross the road in front of, behind and between these vehicles in a dangerous fashion. Grove Road was an unrestricted road with no school signs and no speed limit and as Mr Johnson reported to the managers:

> 'Strange drivers are unaware of the school position and drive at speeds of over 30 m.p.h. and I regret to say that some local drivers are unnecessarily careless.'

In 1965, the PTA wrote to parents:

> 'The indiscriminate parking of cars along the whole frontage of the school creates a dangerous situation due to loss of vision up and down the road. More dangerous still is the use of the front forecourt for driving into and out of to allow children to alight, and the reversing into the main exits to turn around whilst very young children are in close proximity.'

It is extraordinary to think that not until 2011 have gates been locked at school opening and ending time to stop these practices.

Curriculum, Exams and Reports

All children in the junior department sat examinations in core subjects in the summer term and a report was written for each one by their teacher. This did not apply to infants although parental consultations were held throughout the school 2 or 3 times a year. In addition, a dossier was kept by the head with each pupil's Medical Record, teacher's notes, record of other achievements and a photograph. There was no escape.

SONNING COMMON PRIMARY SCHOOL

Name _D. Pound_   Class _4_

School Year ending Summer Term 19_58_

BASIC SUBJECTS			GENERAL SUBJECTS	
English:	Written work	B	Religious Knowledge	B
	Spelling	B	History	B
Reading:	Word recognition	B	Geography	B
	Comprehension	B	Nature Study	B
Arithmetic:	Mental calculations	C	Music	C
	Mechanical methods	B	Physical Education and Games	B
	Problems	B	Art/Crafts	C+

Assessments:

A = Very Good   B = Above Average
C = Average   D = Below Average
E = Very weak and in need of special consideration

A very good year's work. Douglas has done well, and is to be congratulated upon his success at the Selection Examinations.
Best wishes for his future. _____ Class Teacher

This is a very satisfactory report. Douglas is a boy who in all respects has been a satisfactory member of class and school. _____ Headmaster

SCHOOL REPORT - CONFIDENTIAL

The information in this report is confidential between the Headmaster, teachers and parents, and parents may consider it unwise to tell their children of its full content.

To help in the assessment of progress the gradings used are based upon national standards of attainment, and are those now commonly used in Primary Schools. It must be stressed that 'C' gradings are quite satisfactory for a child of average ability.

Douglas Pound final year school report 1958

	TOTAL IN AGE GROUP	ABOVE AVERAGE	LESS THAN 1 YEAR BELOW AVERAGE	1 YEAR OR MORE BELOW AVERAGE	
Infant Transfers	Approximate %'s of Infant children at time of transfer to Junior Department				
1970	86	48	18	20	) 61% – above average) 22% – up to 1 year below average
1971	116	77	25	14	) 17% – 1 year or more below average
	202	125	43	34	
J.1's	At the end of the First Year in Junior Department				
1970	105	61	17	27	) 68% – above average) 15% – up to 1 year below average
1971	93	67	14	12	) 17% – 1 year or more below average
1972	115	84	15	16	)
	313	212	46	55	
J.4's	At time of transfer to Secondary School				
1970	71	67	3	1	) 75% – above average) 19% – up to 1 year below average
1971	63	36	25	2	) 6% – 1 year or more below average
1972	68	49	11	8	)
	202	152	39	11	

Reading Standards 1972

As now, there were concerns about standards. Mr Johnson wrote in 1972:

> 'A very easy way of earning money is to write articles about the low standards of reading in schools under such headings as "Bring out your Illiterates". I would like you to know that in this middle-of-the-road school we have never lost sight of the importance of teaching reading.'

He published his figures for 1972 showing that the majority of children read to average or above average standards. (see opposite)

He was also concerned that pupils should enjoy a broad and balanced curriculum with music, sport, drama and art playing an important role. In January 1974, with school numbers at almost 700 and with 6 temporary classrooms spread around the grounds there was plenty to keep pupils occupied at lunch time and after school – Young Ornithologist's Club, three recorder groups, school orchestra, two chess clubs, drama, voice drama, science club, hockey, athletics for girls, football, stamp club, mini-rugby, care of livestock, gardening and a new children's School Council. The amount of money to be spent on each pupil (capitation) in 1975/77 was £7.50 per pupil per year so the voluntary efforts of adults were vital.

Sex education in schools is always a tricky issue and school managers and now governors have always had to endorse the school's policy. In 1972, Mr Johnson decided not to schedule sex education as a separate subject but to incorporate 'a considerable amount of elementary general biology' to each class according to age. He said there should be a spread of books around and throughout the school which would inform the children and encourage them to ask questions to which they wanted to know the answers. Many members of staff felt the subject was best dealt with at home by enlightened parents but it was recognised that some children would never be informed. Mr Johnson reported to his managers:

> 'It was considered that most of our children, through one teacher or another, or through their parents, were reasonably informed by the time of transfer to secondary school. (Personally, I have grave doubts about this assumption).'

He decided that sex education based upon a 'purely clinical approach' was best avoided, and that 'love, kindness, moral responsibility and a respect for each other' should always be associated with the teaching of human biology.

Sport

In 1958 Mr Johnson instituted the 'House' system for competitions with the two teams, Windsor and Stuart. The Lieutenant Timothy D. Grant Shield was awarded to the House with the most points on Sports Day. (Lieut Grant was killed in action near Arnhem in 1944 and his family donated the shield, for athletics, in his memory.

In the summer term 1958 cricket matches were held with the boundaries defined by colourful posts painted blue and red for Windsor and Stuart. The posts were of course painted by the boys and the flags made by the girls.

The Lady Ottoline Morrell Shield was the trophy awarded for an Oxfordshire football competition and Sonning Common won it on a number of occasions right up to the 1990s.

Morrell Shield winners 1963

Back row: Peter Dolphin, James Minter, Sean Gillott, Derek Boulton, Clive Beer, Martin Jay, Philip Huggins, Bob Pound, Jeffery Pitt
Front row: Donald Townsend, Randy Hayward, Ian Brown, Bryan Slade, Michael Strachan

Morrell Shield winners 1970

Back row: Alan Hayes, Adrian Price, John Wickens, Michael Bell,
Tony Carter, Lee Andrews, Ian Dickens
Front row: Colin Anderson, Martin Swain, Simon Wright, Andrew Lambert,
Grant Beverley, Patrick Deighan, Stuart Hargreaves

This team won the Morrell Shield in 1970, beating Wheatley in the final. As a treat, the winning team were taken to see Reading play Stockport in a midweek match which Reading won 8 – 0.

football 1967

Back row: David Allison, Michael Gale, Graham Stevens, ?, Gary Peedell,
Robert Allison, Ian Pearson, Kevin Lilleystone, Malcolm Tutty
Middle row: Nigel Blodwell, Graham Woodley, Derek Stansbury,
Neil Blodwell, Stephen Hudson
Front row: Neil Kirby, Stephen Salt

From 1968 or perhaps earlier, football and netball were played after school and football teams (school and visiting) used the school field on Saturdays. Mr Johnson commented:

> *'We continue to play our regular "enemies" namely, Henley, Goring, Woodcote and Micklands at football and netball whenever possible'.*

Mr Pitson ran the South Oxfordshire Schools Football Association on Saturday mornings, based at Sonning Common because it boasted the best pitch in the area. The school was fortunate to have on the staff Mr Colin Roper who was a qualified F.A. coach and who, along with Mr Carter and enthusiastic parents set up the Saturday afternoon football club. Mr and Mrs England helped with the organisation and with the making of goal posts and bib sewing. At one time 112 boys played football over two sessions. Saturday football continued for many years and, as far as we know, no girl ever asked to join.

Not all sports at the school were of such a highly competitive nature. Here is Dorothy Wickens (in swimsuit) in the egg and spoon race in 1969.

Egg and Spoon race 1969

Football 1973

Back row: Robert ?, Stuart Mc Culley, ?, Christopher Harris, Nicholas Pitson, ?, Trevor Howard, Stanley Szymans
Front row: Anthony Murphy, Martin Payne, Mark Lambert, ?, Graham Morgan

Netball 1976-77

Back row: ?, ?, Lucy Oldridge, Corina Gay
Front row: Sue McCulley, Hannah Palmer, Mrs Badnell , Claire Foxley, Sally Hankin, Gemma Best

Back row: Mrs Brodie, Mr Beadle, Mr Henderson, Mrs Morgan
Front row: ? Mrs Arch, Mr Carter, Mr Pitson, Mrs Pitt, Mrs Harris, Mrs Twyman

This photograph from about 1970 shows a staff cricket team that played against the children. It was taken at the bottom of the playing field and anyone who has seen that area in recent years may recognise the houses which are in Elm Court and the tiny shrubs that are now huge trees hiding the houses completely.

The Swimming Pool

Prior to 1970 groups of children were taken to Turners Court (Benson) for swimming lessons. (Turners Court is described in the book, Benson – a century of change by J. Burtt and P. Clarke as *'a reformatory for youths who had crossed with society'*). Mrs Sue Green (Hayden) remembers going there mostly because children could visit the tuck shop after their swim and she especially enjoyed the long, red strings of liquorice that were available.

The school 'trainer' pool was funded by parents and opened in 1970 in no small part due to the efforts of Mr Pitson who organised a 200 club to raise funds. The cost of the pool was about £6000. Pye Estates who built houses in Westleigh Drive and Lea Road donated £3000 towards the cost. At this stage, only junior age pupils had a weekly lesson but the pool was also proving to be a great amenity to the adult population of the village. Some parents objected to their children being forced as non-swimmers to take to the water but the school insisted. Mrs Joyce Hargreaves and the trustees were thanked for their contribution of £300 to the school (used to purchase reference books) which was raised from the proceeds of swimming lessons. Other trustees were Mr Foster, Mr Morgan, Mr Johnson (headmaster) and Alderman Mrs de Pass (chair of managers).

Punishment

Times were changing in the world of corporal punishment. Canings were now generally witnessed by a second teacher. Mr Johnson makes few entries to the punishment book and most are accompanied by greater detail than ever before. For example, Z. Mikosz received 3 strokes on the seat for *'causing continual trouble to class teacher after repeated warnings by teacher and Headmaster'*. Mr Johnson comments:

> *'This boy has ability but is in danger of going wrong. It is hoped that this punishment will act as a timely warning'.*

Mr Johnson ruled with a 'virtual' iron hand. Children were very frightened when asked by a teacher to stand outside the classroom door. If Mr Johnson came walking down the corridor and found them they knew they were in trouble. He walked very quietly but, as former pupil Richard Green remembers, his shoes tended to squeak and he would always be humming. That hum struck fear into naughty children. Mrs Morgan (teacher at SCPS 1966-1983) remembers that he used to make pupils stand so that the sun was in their eyes which put them at a disadvantage – a trick he retained from his days as a fighter pilot when it was German pilots he was disadvantaging. In his own words:

> *'... most children, disciplined within a framework of kindness and justice, are happy children and the more likely to master the skills and rules of good living'.*

Robert Austin has the dubious honour of being the last pupil caned at Sonning Common Primary School on 30th October 1964. He received one stroke for *'Bullying nine year old girl only one week after warning given to whole school at which he was present.'*

In 1965, Mr Johnson made the final record in the Punishment Book.

> *'Corporal punishment by use of the cane abolished by my own decision as it no longer seems necessary, but if ever I thought it was necessary I should not hesitate to re-introduce its use.'*

His attitude to punishment was not without humour. He reported to the managers in 1972 that he had seen some "lines" on a master's desk which read - **'I must not become inebriated by the exuberance of my own verbosity.'**

He also wrote:

> *'During the past few weeks I corrected a boy for "forgetting" his games kit so often. Without consultation I learn that he has since written to the Prime Minister asking why games must be played in school. I understand that he has received an answer. The boy is now due to see me again as his general standard of letter writing is still much below standard and must be improved.'*

Children who did well were rewarded. On his desk, Mr Johnson had a jar of sweets and those sent to him to show good work were allowed to dip their hand into the jar and take a sweet.

Parents

Mr Johnson supported the PTA and welcomed the additional resources their fundraising gave to the school. The PTA arranged social events and lectures and in 1965, 120 parents attended a meeting to hear about new secondary arrangements. However, he kept parents firmly in their place, which was outside the gates. When, in 1971 a small group of parents suggested, through the PTA, that children should be allowed to bring a packed lunch to school, they were firmly told that this was no concern of theirs.

He made himself available on Monday and Wednesday afternoons for consultations and at other times by appointment but made it clear that:

> *'Frivolous complaints or irresponsible criticism of staff are not tolerated.'*

Teachers were not in contact with parents on a daily basis. Children were left at the school gates by their parents in the morning and even after there was an entrance in Lea Road infants were escorted to the gate by their teacher and collected from there. Parents were not encouraged onto the premises and teachers were:

> *'approachable for good purpose through the proper channels but need not be available to callers except by arrangement'.*

Trips

From the beginning of Mr Johnson's headship, trips out of school were important, as were visitors coming into school. In 1959 groups travelled to the Tower of London, the Natural History Museum, the Science Museum, the Commonwealth Institute, the Victoria and Albert Museum, London Airport, Peppard Chest Hospital and to the cinema for films relevant to the curriculum.

In 1972 Mr Beadle took his class to Hythe, Kent for a week's study, including a day trip to France and Mr Pitson took his class to Wales for a week's hill walking and pony trekking. Other places visited include the Wildfowl Trust, Slimbridge, Berkeley Castle, bus/steamer trip on Thames, The Icknield Way and theatres in Oxford. Travelling theatre groups performed for pupils in school and visitors from overseas were welcomed.

Music and Drama

Music and drama were seen as important parts of a balanced curriculum and the school was fortunate to have some talented teachers who were able to produce plays and concerts. Christmas concerts for parents were held every year along with Harvest Festivals and poppies were always sold for Remembrance Day. In December 1968 there were 100 children learning to play the recorder. A junior school orchestra operated as an extra-curricular activity. In the late 1960s Christmas concerts for the juniors were held in the long corridor with the audience of parents in the classrooms. Mr Johnson would stand at one end conducting the proceedings with Mr Pitson at the other end of the corridor copying the headmaster's conducting.

In the summer term 1970 there was a combined schools musical festival at Chiltern Edge, 'More Sounds of Music' (J3 and J4), including 'Creation Jazz' by Gwyn Arch whose wife Mrs Jane Arch had been a member of staff since January and whose children David and Jonathan were pupils. Mrs Diana Bean presented a concert of songs and recorder by children in J1 and J2 (Years 3 and 4).

Mr Johnson backstage at a school production

The 'Studio'

Children with Special Needs have always been supported at the school even if the words used to describe them have not always been as we would now think appropriate. In the 50s and early 60s there was enough space for a separate class taught by Mr Lockwood but as pressure for classroom space became greater this was not possible. During Mr Johnson's absence (through illness) in 1970, Mr Carter oversaw the 'Studio' project as a sort of welcome back for the headmaster. The 'studio' was a small caravan equipped for 6 children and an adult to work quietly and at their own pace. It was sited, once planning permission was granted, on what is now the staff carpark and cost around £185. It was paid for by the proceeds from a Home Produce Market Stall, and the encashing of over 118 completed books of Green Shield Stamps. It contained 'sophisticated electrical equipment' – one Phillips cassette tape recorder, one Bell and Howell 'Language master' and six stack-away stools. The help of many was noted but particularly that of Mr and Mrs Fieldhouse who were responsible for painting the external surface and installing fixtures and fittings.

Caretaking and Catering

In September 1959 Mr H T Smith ('Brusher' Smith) became caretaker, replacing Mr Wade. He was partially disabled having only one arm and a prosthetic second arm with a hook at the end. There was some concern when he was employed that he might not be able to manage but manage he did for many years. Brusher Smith remained caretaker beyond the normal retirement age of 65. He was replaced in 1973 by Mr Patrick Butler (referred to in the Managers' Minutes as "young" Mr Butler) who remains caretaker to this day and is the first and only caretaker to live in the school house.

The school canteen (demolished in 2003 to make way for the present Year 6 classrooms) was the domain of Mrs Wynn until 1961 when she was replaced by Mrs Joy. By May 1962, 200 meals were being served daily to children in facilities that accommodated 180 in two full sittings of 90. No child was allowed to bring a packed lunch – it was school dinner or home for all pupils. By December 1964, the dining facilities could no longer cope with the number of diners and Mr Johnson decided not to allow any more children to stay for school lunch. He instituted a waiting list but gave priority to pupils living over 20 minutes walking distance from the school. In 1967 he was forced to accept new diners only on presentation of a medical certificate. He wrote:

'As children leave the school, new diners will be admitted according to their place on the list. Children who are not regular diners and who bring dinner money to school will by necessity be sent home at lunch time.'

Those who went home for lunch came back to school under very strict conditions. Mrs Sue Green (Hayden) recalls that if you came back before the appointed time you were not allowed to join the dinner children at play but must stand with your back to the wall until it was time to go into class. When the whistle blew at any time of day to announce the start of the lessons, pupils stood still and silent until their class teacher's name was called, at which point they would silently file in.

Once the new infant building was opened it was possible to cater for greater numbers. In 1968 with 2 kitchens each providing meals for two sittings of children, 416 children were provided with a daily hot meal. The cost of a school meal in 1963 was one shilling (5p), in 1971 it was 12p and in 2012 it is £2.10. More than 500 children were catered for daily in the two canteens with two sittings in each.

Health

Throughout the period of Mr Johnson's headship there were the usual outbreaks of mumps, measles, chickenpox and German measles which could have a great effect on daily class attendance but no school closures as in the early years. In 1970, whilst Mr Johnson was absent through illness himself, there was an outbreak of dysentery. Mr Carter, as acting head, wrote to parents urging them to ensure that children followed the same rigorous hygiene procedures at home as had been instituted at school. Bowls of disinfectant were placed near to washbasins and children were to use these before washing their hands thoroughly with soap and water. They must rinse away the soap with running water and use only disposable paper towels which must be disposed of correctly. Mr Carter advised:

'If your child has "the trots" contact your local doctor.'

Weather

The winter of 1962/63 was one of the harshest on record (my own great grandmother came to stay for Christmas and was still with us for her birthday in April). In the school log book Mr Johnson wrote:

'Late Christmas day it began to snow and by Boxing Day two to three feet of snow had fallen'.

Mr Johnson reported that almost all his staff attended the day before term was due to start along with a volunteer group of pupils and ex-pupils, to clear paths through deep snow and drifts to all main entrances and exits. He wrote:

> 'Many children entered school through narrow paths which towered above their heads on either side'.

The catering staff attended early to check equipment and take in supplies and the caretaker worked daily with no Christmas holiday and no free weekend since before Christmas to ensure that heating and water would be available. Remarkably, on the first day of term attendance was 87% rising to 94% the following week when conditions were just as bad. Mr Johnson requested an additional day's holiday for everyone during Henley Regatta Week as a reward for all their efforts.

However, by the middle of January the school was forced to close because of frozen main water pipes. Although they managed one day without mains water by carrying water to school in containers, meals and toilets could not be provided and the school had to close.

Library

Under Mr Johnson a Public Library was established in the school hall (half of the building where the library is now housed) and was open to the public on Wednesday afternoon, Monday and Friday evenings. At other times the school used the library area. Mr Johnson reported on its popularity:

> 'It can fairly be said that the general public are now a disturbance factor on Wednesday afternoons. I have often been tempted to place a notice which says "Quiet, please, school at work!"'

In May 1961, approval was given for the use of 100 feet of schoolhouse garden for a library and planning permission was sought. The terrapin was constructed in 1965 but the library was housed in the school for some time after that.

1961 – Henry Wickens in the library

By 1966, the pressure for pupil space was so great that the library could no longer be accommodated during the school day so was open on Saturdays, allowing the school to use the library space at other times.

Dobinson Paddock

Mrs Dobinson was a school manager and her two daughters kept horses on what is now called the 'Dobinson Paddock', the area beyond the main school playing field. The Dobinsons were asked in 1951 if they would sell the parcel of land to the school but they declined. Professor and Mrs Dobinson received a nominal sum of money when they gave the 1.98 acres of land to the school in 1966 with the agreement that the land would never be built on.

Mr Johnson wrote:

> *'I shall name the area The Dobinson Paddock and retain as many of the trees, and as much of the natural hedgerow as possible to try and maintain in the midst of a sea of masonry one piece of the countryside.'*

This approach has continued to this day with the establishment of Forest School in recent years (see Chapter 15).

Falling Numbers and industrial action

In the second half of the 1970s there was a financial crisis nationally which led to cuts in education as well as all other government departments. Numbers on roll were falling but cuts led to larger classes and no money for 'rising 5s' to be admitted to school. The year 1976 was a difficult one for the headteacher with many groups within the school considering industrial action. NUPE (National Union for Public Employees) advised its members to take action against cutbacks in cleaning services, earnings and deteriorating working conditions.

Most teachers took industrial action against Oxfordshire's cuts in education budget by withdrawing their services on Tuesday 21st September 1976 for the morning session.

Mr Johnson's reaction:

> *'I refuse to lose control of this school, even if it must be closed by <u>me</u> for reasons beyond <u>my</u> control as Headteacher.'*

Mr Johnson's retirement

In 1965 Mr Johnson told his school managers that he:

> *...never sought publicity but preferred the school's reputation to be upheld by word of mouth. No reporter ever invited to the school, no speech days or prize givings, no exhibitions ...*

He continued with this policy to the end of his headship when he resigned along with Miss Evans, Mr Beadle and Mrs Johnson (his wife and school secretary) to finish in August 1977.

He said:

> *'No speeches. No farewells. Just no nothing. I have had the great privilege of being Headmaster of this school for twenty years. It has been my great privilege to be a servant to this community and its children in particular.'*

There was no party and no big send-off – a tiny paragraph in The Henley Standard announced his retirement along with those of teachers from other local schools.

Chapter Eight

A Family's story – Joyce Wise (Towse)

*M*any families have attended Sonning Common Primary School through generations. The Towse family is one of these.

Here is Joyce Towse in 1957. Joyce enrolled at Sonning Common County Primary School (locally known as Grove Road School) when she was seven. Her sisters Gloria and Jeannette and her brother Colin also attended Grove Road School. Joyce remembers Mr Enever as headteacher and then Mr Johnson. She also recalls Mrs Clayton, Mr Lockwood (Father Christmas), Mr Higgins (smelt of mothballs), Miss Evans, Mrs Evans and Mrs Fisher.

Her school memories are not really happy ones. Joyce enjoyed art and history and particularly disliked needlework. She was always cold despite the school cardigans and jumpers knitted by her mother. Of course, the toilets were outside at the end of the playground and the wind whistled around the building which was partly open to the elements. Joyce remembers feeling very small in the large buildings.

Joyce's favourite teacher was Mr Lockwood because he was gentle. Her friends included June and May Huggins, Val Parsons, Joan Wynne and the Hendry girls. The girls played hopscotch and skipping and the boys played marbles.

June and May Huggins

Mr Johnson is remembered as being so strict that children would hide when they saw him but the most terrifying figure was Mr Webber, the school attendance officer. He would visit the families of non-attending children and always carried his briefcase under his arm. His car would be seen around the village.

Joyce married Malcolm Wise and had two children, Craig and Kim and in 1976 she returned to the school herself as a kitchen assistant. She was interviewed by Mr Johnson in his office which was by the Grove Road entrance (the foyer of the computer suite). Joyce was very, very nervous at the prospect of seeing Mr Johnson again and he did not help by answering her timid knock with 'Come in, Towse'.

However, he was teasing her, she got the job and has been in post ever since, latterly as head cook.

Joyce's son Craig Wise started school in 1975 and his sister Kim in 1977.

Kim Wise attended the school between 1977 and 1982 when firstly Mr Sharman was headteacher and then Mr Pitson. Unlike her mother, Kim looks back on her days at the school with great affection:

'I never again in my schooldays felt the safety and freedom to be myself'.

Kim loved learning history and her favourite teacher of that subject was Mr Bain. She recalls that the local community and residents were part of lessons which made the whole experience come alive for her. Not only that, he taught her a mnemonic for the points of the compass – (N)ever (E)at (S)hredded (W)heat and she has never forgotten it!

Residential school trips have long been a feature of school life and Kim's J4 (Year6) trip was to Swanage. She remembers feeling very grown up and daring especially when an impromptu tap dancing lesson was conducted at midnight – Kim concedes that although this felt like midnight it was probably closer to 9 o'clock. Her fellow dancers were Clare Borland, Sarah Northway, Sarah and Lindsey Griffiths and Andrena Martin.

Mr Bain and Mrs Morgan ready for the school trip

Other treasured memories include storytime in the Dobinson Paddock on summer days when it was too hot to be inside, Mr Arch helping with the musical arrangement for a production of Joseph and his Technicolour Dreamcoat and Mrs Fieldhouse's fashionable scarves worn in the same production.

Kim's son Archie Scobey started school in 2005 and Kittie followed in 2006. They echo their mother's love of history and school day trips to the Imperial War Museum have been particularly enjoyed. Residential trips – no longer just the privilege of children in their final school year – are recalled as times of huge fun and friendship.

The only unhappy times remembered by these children are when favourite teachers and friends have left the school. Kittie, always a very cheerful and positive girl says:

'Every moment has been happy'.

For this family, school has become a much happier and positive experience over the generations.

Archie and Kittie Scobey

Chapter Nine
Mr R. H. Sharman (1978 – 1982)

$\mathcal{M}$r Stuart Pitson served one term as acting headteacher before Mr Rod Sharman became the fourth headteacher of Sonning Common Primary School in January 1978. His tenure was brief- only five years- but eventful.

He came from a small village school, Horspath, and his ideas were very far from the traditional ideas of the previous headmaster. Mr Sharman was young and forward-looking, typical of the headteachers Oxfordshire was looking for in the 1980s. The rest of the staff remained much the same and, for the most part, were ready to embrace new ideas, though not without discussion and, if necessary, compromise.

Mr Sharman introducing the Band of the Irish Guards – 1979

The 5 years of Mr Sharman's headship were at a time when the school roll was rapidly declining as families became established in the village and their children moved on to secondary education. The spectre of redeployment or redundancy shadowed each summer term as did reductions in the hours of ancillary and office staff. The number of pupils decreased from 482 in September 1978 to 271 in September 1983. The school with no space now had rooms (and teachers) to spare. This enabled some creative use of space and extensions to some classrooms by removing internal walls and allowing rooms to be used by other groups. Mr Sharman had a firm belief that the best way to group children was in mixed age groups (family grouping) and he slowly moved the school towards this. He decided, as the teacher most used to family grouping, that for one year he would teach a class himself and ask Mr Pitson (deputy head) to take over the administrative aspects of the school. Pupils were grouped so that infants would have the same teacher for their first two years in school and juniors would be grouped with 7 to 9 year olds together and 9 to 11 year olds together. Two junior classes were moved across to the infant building. This was accepted by the staff and parents after discussion and became the pattern for many years. Only quite recently has the school reverted to classes where children are grouped by age.

Teaching staff in January 1979 were as follows:

Infants were grouped in 2s and named after the nearby trees.

Cherry House –	Mrs M Choules (previously Mills)
	Mrs V Evans /Mrs H Wilson
Oak House –	Mrs J Dodd
	Mrs J Welch
Poplar House –	Mrs A Edwards
	Mrs C Abbey
J1 (year 3) –	Mrs D Trainor, Mr D Hansen
J2 (year 4) –	Mrs J Harris, Mrs M Fieldhouse, Mrs S Badnell
J3 (year 5) –	Mrs J Kendal, Mr W Bain, Mrs J Arch
J4 (year 6) –	Mrs F Morgan, Mrs D Bean, Mr S Pitson

Mrs P Twyman and Mrs M Gwyther took Mr Pitson's class in the first term

The process began of encouraging everyone to think of themselves as one school, separated only by a playground. Previously, the school had been clearly divided, even the finishing time was not the same for both departments. Soon a shared staffroom brought everyone together at least twice a day, assemblies for all were held in the infant hall and then the junior department gave up their mid-afternoon breaktime in order to finish at 3.30 as the infants did.

Link with Bishopswood Special School

In the Year of the Disabled, 1981, a class of seven pupils from Bishopswood Special School in Horspond Road moved into a spare classroom following many visits and much discussion. Their teacher and classroom helper came too. Within a term and a half there was some integration of the children in to mainstream classes and co-operation between staff to share expertise. A second class was established in 1983, thus enabling the children to spend all their primary years in one school.

Premises

Over many years, the school managers (from 1980 they became Governors) had to concern themselves with matters lavatorial and the matter of outside toilets was raised many times. In May 1978 a group of parents petitioned the Local Education Authority (LEA) to remove or at least stop the use of the playground lavatories but, as the chair of managers reported, concerns had already been ongoing for 20 years and were not to be resolved until much later. (The outdoor toilets were still being used in1995!) Local doctors also became involved with Dr Tom Stewart writing to the LEA to protest about the condition of the facilities:

> -'there are no hand washing facilities whatsoever, although these toilets are used by children before meals
>
> -they are not completely covered in and the roof leaks
>
> -many of the toilets have ancient wooden seats, most of them peppered with woodworm and some of them have actually disintegrated and splintered
>
> -the toilets freeze in bad weather and cannot be used'

However, because of the number of junior children and the small number of indoor toilets the situation was to remain the same although some improvement was made including sink installation for pupils to wash their hands under cover. Teachers remember 'patrolling' these toilets at playtimes and they were grim but it was useful to save children having to go inside at breaktime where they were less easy to supervise.

The second canteen (demolished in 2003 to make way for the Year 6 classrooms) closed as a catering facility in 1980 because the number of pupils taking dinner could be accommodated in the infant building. The old canteen could now be used for craft work and children's cooking. By October 1981 there had been a change of policy on packed lunches and 150 – 160 children now brought their own lunch to school. In 1982 Mrs Iris Ockendon was school cook – Mr Sharman described her as a person who always had a smile for everyone.

Mrs Ockendon

Parents in school

Mr Sharman encouraged parents to help in school with swimming, library cataloguing and local trips and made a room available for their use. He held meetings for parents to discuss changes in their children's curriculum – 'The place of the environment in children's learning' and 'How do children learn to calculate?' were topics tackled early on. He also ended the practice of teachers escorting their class to the gate at the end of each day and parents were now allowed through the gates and onto the playgrounds. School uniform became a thing of the past in this era.

Meetings for parents before their child started school were another innovation giving parents the chance to look around the school and children to meet their teacher and spend time in their new classroom before starting school on the second day of term.

Playgroup

In 1978 a new building for the playgroup was proposed to replace the 'temporary' Elliott building. Mr Sharman spoke at the playgroup's AGM and their leaders spent time in school. By 1979 the old terrapins were no longer needed by the school because the number of pupils was falling and the buildings could be used by the playgroup. In 1981 the Local Education Authority took away the Elliott buildings for use by another school but agreed to rent the land at a low cost. Six thousand pounds was needed for a new building to be put up. This was raised and the building opened later that year.

Curriculum

Mr Sharman wanted children to learn from 'first hand' experience and not from text book based learning and encouraged the use of the school environment and locality for learning. The school pond was built in 1980 by Mr Butler and Mr Allum who was caretaker in the infant building. There was also a poultry unit containing ducks and chickens, two greenhouses, a small garden, a wasteland area for wildlife and numerous nesting boxes in the grounds. An aviary was constructed in the courtyard adjoining the infant hall. Exercise books were frowned upon and children in the juniors began to make their own bookcovers and used loose leafed sheets sewn together to create (in some cases) mini works of art. Italic handwriting also became the order of the day which required training for staff as well as children.

Display of children's work was meticulous. All classrooms had display areas created with huge rolls of corrugated card – up to six feet high and as wide as any wall. Work samples and art work were attached to the background with dressmakers' pins which had a habit of falling out regularly. Drawing pins were outlawed completely and staple guns were unheard of in schools.

Art work was displayed all over the school and the children achieved a high standard through the efforts of their class teacher and specialist help from Mrs Pauline Twyman. Everyone became used to a succession of visitors from all over the world coming to see what was happening in a 1980s Oxfordshire school.

An historical topic would often be concluded with a 'dressing up' day.

Mrs Fieldhouse and class – Victorian Day 1981

The concept of in-house training was introduced and staff took part in discussion groups and workshops as well as the usual staff meetings. The first two topics to be discussed were mathematics and handwriting, closely followed by bookcrafts, language development and reading.

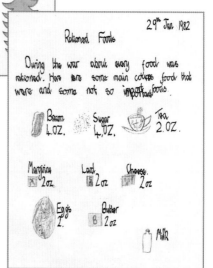

1982 – beautiful italic writing – Mrs Morgan's class

History project work by Richard Curzon (Mrs Kendal's class)

The school obtained its first minibus (funded mainly by the PTA) in 1979. Residential school trips were no longer for the oldest children only and trips were followed by displays of children's work which were open to the public. Trips were not all about learning in a different environment – this looks like a fun disco.

J4 (Year 6) trip to Yenworthy 1982

In 1982 a group of pupils and staff went on an exchange trip to Tuscon, Arizona where they stayed with families and spent time in the school attended by the pupils.

In 1981 Mr Sharman, along with primary schools advisor John Coe, took a group of 20 children to Luxembourg to work in Luxembourg's schools, observed by Luxembourgish teachers. This innovative move was widely reported both locally and nationally.

1981 Luxembourg

A school holiday scrapbook

By JUNE WILKINSON

■ Off we go! Sailing away on the ferry.

TWENTY Thames Valley children have just returned from the school outing of a lifetime.

Together with their headmaster Mr Rod Sharman the youngsters — from Sonning Common Primary School — were invited to go to Luxembourg for a week.

They went as guests of the country's ministry of education for a study visit.

The Luxembourg government has been looking at education methods in Britain and, over the last 18 months, Luxembourg teachers have been visiting schools in Oxfordshire.

Also on the trip were Mr John Coe, senior primary adviser to the county, and Mrs Yvonne Ward, a primary adviser.

The children travelled by boat and train to Luxembourg.

They spent the mornings out and about in the Duchy, while in the afternoons classes were held at the teacher training centre so Luxembourg teachers could study British classroom methods.

One highlight of the trip was a visit to the European Parliament building.

The Luxembourg minister of education and the British Ambassador both spent time with the children — 10 boys and 10 girls.

And in the evenings the youngsters were free to meet Luxembourg children of their age.

Mr Sharman said: "With the exception of getting caught in a blizzard on the way home, it was an extremely interesting and enjoyable trip, and the children have got plenty to tell their classmates."

■ And here we are in Luxembourg — doing a bit of sketching.

■ This is one of our trips — to look at a castle.

■ Here's how we started our day — with a fine breakfast.

Henley Standard

Mr Sharman continued the school policy of supporting less able pupils but said also *'we must push our more able children'*. For the first time infant children received a written report from their teacher in the summer term. He also proposed that records held by the school about each individual pupil should be available for parents to see and no longer kept confidential.

OXFORDSHIRE COUNTY COUNCIL
SONNING COMMON PRIMARY SCHOOL

Name...Michael Woodfrey............ Class...Mrs. Chandler.

Report for the School Year ending July 19 81.

Michael is a reliable and responsible member of the class. He is confident and self-sufficient. He generally works hard but can be distracted from his work by other children.

He must develop a more critical attitude to his own written work because it tends to be repetitive and unimaginative. At times Michael's writing is less than careful. His reading has progressed steadily and he enjoys reading for pleasure.

Michael's real forte is mathematics. He loves a challenging assignment and progresses eagerly. He manipulates figures with some confidence and can transfer his knowledge to problem solving situations.

Class Teacher ...Melanie Chandler.. Headmaster ...R.H. Sharman.

If you have any comments to make on your child's report please use this tear-off slip and return it to the school.

Mrs. Abbey will be Michael's teacher next term

Name of Child .... Class ....

This is a report written in 1981. The teacher criticised Michael's written work which seems a bit cheeky as her writing is shocking. In her defence, this was in the days before most teachers had computers and, as his surname begins with W, she had probably already written thirty. He does know that it is being reproduced here.

Technology

This is what Mr Sharman had to say about computers in classrooms in 1981, a time when there were none in the school:

> *'schools must start thinking now of the ways in which it (computer) can help children in their development. If we do not take this step I fear the computer will merely replace the text book and a child will talk into a computer instead of reading a text book. The rate of growth of the microchip is quite phenomenal.'*

He saw the computer as an efficient way to store information but no substitute for the contact between adult and child which led to creative learning. The first classroom computer was installed in 1982. The LEA decided to provide Research Machine 480Z to all its schools with the government providing half funding at £460 per machine. Fortunately, as a pilot school Sonning Common did not have to pay anything at all.

Concerts and plays

School productions continued to be important to the life of the school and, during this period, included Pirates of Penzance, The Golden Legend, Pinocchio, Joseph and his Amazing Technicolour Dreamcoat, Daniel Jazz, and The Phantom Tollbooth.

PTA

The PTA was as active as ever in raising funds for the school. A novel way of advertising the Christmas Bazaar was found in 1982 –

Ian Larden, Joanne Smith, Jane Hiscock, Tereena Jibbon and Debbie Lambert proudly display the specially printed Christmas Cards designed by members of the junior school at Grove Road Primary School's bazaar on Saturday.

Double-headed fair made £500 for school

When Sonning Common Primary School's annual craft fair and Christmas bazaar took place on Saturday afternoon, the old town hall was filled with all manner of crafts, including wood turning, pottery, jewellery and soft toys, while inside the new hall the numerous stalls in the bazaar did a roaring trade.

Meanwhile, Father Christmas was the centre of attraction for the younger visitors.

The Christmas fair, the last presided over by headmaster Rod Sharman, who is leaving at the end of the term to take up a post with the Inner London Education Authority, made a profit of around £500.

PTA member Clive Mills said that the money was needed to make improvements to the swimming pool and to put towards the purchase of a new minibus.

James Gross (left) and Nick Phillips drummed up business for the Grove Road Primary School bazaar with their eye-catching sandwich boards.

Henley Standard

Sport

Sonning Common School has always had a proud sporting tradition which continued through Mr Sharman's time at the school although he was perhaps not so keen on the competitive aspects.

SONNING COMMON PRIMARY SCHOOL

SPORTS CERTIFICATE

FIRST

INFANT SPORTS TEAM 9

JONATHAN GOULD, HANNAH WATKINS, TIM BOYCE, REBECCA REES, ROBERT HATCH, STEVEN BRAISHER, SARAH WOODWARD

This certificate shows how the infants adapted their sports to put greater emphasis on teamwork rather than individual prowess.

Hockey
1979/1980

Back row: Debbie Samuel, Juliette Cottrell, Fiona Gordon, Sarah Palmer, Mary Dodd, Joanne Catt
Front row: Caroline Thompson, Karen Doughty, Clare Brightwell, Jackie Farina, Tara Cole

Boys rugby team 1981-82

Back row: Simon Gregory, Gregory Lyons, Robert Green, Jonathan Appleby, Boyd McAfee, Robin Fenwick, Michael Curzon
Front row: Johnny Hobbs, John Palmer, Neil Halstead, Richard Curzon, Alastair Jenkinson, Neil Halliday, Toby Cole

Nicholas Phillips and Ian Skinner competing in a distance race on Junior Sports Day.

Falklands War

Sadly, during this conflict another name was added to the plaque commemorating fallen soldiers who had been pupils at the school:

Pte F. Slough 1982, 2 Paras

When Mr Sharman resigned he quoted this poem by Dorothy Law Nolte as one which epitomised and was the corner stone of his work with children –

CHILDREN LEARN WHAT THEY LIVE
Dorothy Law Nolte (1972)

If a child lives with criticism,
he learns to condemn.
If a child lives with hostility,
he learns to fight.
If a child lives with fear,
he learns to be apprehensive.
If a child lives with pity,
he learns to feel sorry for himself.
If a child lives with ridicule,
he learns to be shy.
If a child lives with jealousy,
he learns what envy is.
If a child lives with shame,
he learns to feel guilty.
If a child lives with encouragement,
he learns to be confident.
If a child lives with tolerance,
he learns to be patient.
If a child lives with praise,
he learns to be appreciative.

If a child lives with acceptance,
he learns to love.
If a child lives with approval,
he learns to like himself.
If a child lives with recognition,
he learns that it is good to have a goal.
If a child lives with sharing,
he learns about generosity.
If a child lives with honesty and fairness,
he learns what truth and justice are.
If a child lives with security,
he learns to have faith in himself and
in those about him.
If a child lives with friendliness,
he learns that the world is a nice
place in which to live.
If you live with serenity,
your child will live with peace of mind.

With what is your child living?

Mr Sharman left the school in December 1982 to take up a post in the Inner London Education Authority (ILEA) and was replaced by Mr Stuart Pitson.

Chapter Ten
Mr S. M. Pitson (1983 – 1992)

r Pitson became the school's sixth headteacher in January 1983 having been at the school (apart from a year as acting head at Crowmarsh School) since 1965. There were 345 pupils on roll in 11 classes. (One new teacher joined the staff this term – Mrs Jackie Million who is currently the Chair of Governors.) The number of children on roll continued to drop and Mr Pitson and his deputy, Mrs Jane Arch had to consider how to organise the school for the years to come. The LEA made a simple calculation – number of children divided by 32 equals number of teaching staff. Unfortunately, calculations within school were never that simple as children refused to be born within groups of exactly 32.

Numbers continued to fall and in September 1986 (by which time Mr Steve Edwards had become deputy headteacher) the roll was 232 children in 9 classes.

Mr S.M. Pitson

Legislation and changes to the curriculum

In the 1960s and 1970s, schools and headteachers had had relative freedom to organise the curriculum as they wished but this was to change. The Chief Education Officer in Oxfordshire at this time was Tim Brighouse and he was quick to realise that greater accountability was on its way. In 1984 the LEA introduced its own process of four-yearly school evaluations. Although prepared by the school, these were monitored closely by a Primary Adviser and a team from the LEA. These led to pupil profiling and a School Development Plan. Governors and the headteacher prepared an annual report for parents and a meeting for parents was held to discuss the report. Mr Pitson records his disappointment at the number of parents that attended; just 18 one year and eventually dropping so low that the report was simply distributed and written questions invited.

The Education Reform Act 1988 held great significance for all primary school as it heralded the introduction of the National Curriculum. Training courses followed for teachers and governors who, in turn, held meetings with parents to explain the new curriculum. Children were to be grouped in Key Stages and at each stage a number of educational objectives were to be achieved. Key Stage 1 encompassed children in years 1 and 2 and Key Stage 2, children from years 3 to 6 (age 7-11). These would be common to all state schools. A common syllabus was seen as necessary because it was a pupil's right to have access to the same agreed body of knowledge. In order to test this knowledge, statutory Standard Assessment Tasks (SATs) were also introduced nationally, in July 1991 for all 7 year olds and in 1995 for all 11 year olds.

In July 1990 Mr Pitson wrote –

> 'My staff have been under constant pressure as a result of the New National Curriculum but have worked tirelessly. Someone, somewhere is responsible for the pressure and more is to come.'

In-service training days (5 each year) were introduced for all teachers and were known as Baker Days after the Minister for Education at the time.

Also in 1988, Local management of Schools (LMS) was introduced which gave schools financial control over their budget. Suddenly, headteachers and their Governors, especially their finance committee, had to be accountants and manage a large but, with every year, diminishing budget. Each year brought gloomy news about a reduced budget and battles had to be fought to improve the school's allocation of funds.

Premises

This plan shows how building use changed over time.

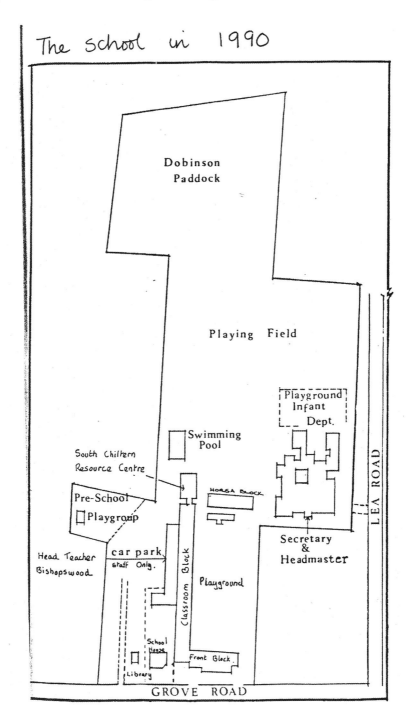

The school in 1990

Dobinson Paddock

Playing Field

Playground Infant Dept.

Swimming Pool

South Chiltern Resource Centre

HORSA BLOCK

Pre-School
Playgroup

LEA ROAD

Head Teacher Bishopswood

car park
Staff Only.

Classroom Block

Playground

Secretary & Headmaster

School House

Library

Front Block

GROVE ROAD

By 1988 ramping for wheelchairs was in place and plans made for a head's office and secretary's office so that in the 1990 plan we can see that Bishopswood School had moved from its site in Horspond Road and was now completely integrated locationally on the Sonning Common campus, with the nursery class at Valley Road, Henley and the senior class at Chiltern Edge.

For a while, the old canteen was used as a Railway Club, run by Mr George Allum who had been the caretaker in the infant block but was, by this time, too poorly to work. He wanted to maintain his link with the school and so set up his model railway.

In 1988 the old canteen had become the South Chiltern Resource Centre and was the base for the Special Needs Advisory Support teachers (SNASTs) with Christine Davies as technician. The rear part of the building where the actual cooking had taken place was still used for art work and had a children's cookery area.

These two girls (Anna Irwin and Jessica Rowley) enjoying a skip around the junior playground demonstrate how little the exterior of the junior school had changed in decades.

Mr Pitson was a keen photographer of school events and also introduced annual class, team and staff photos.

Here are the first and last staff pictures whilst Mr Pitson was headteacher.

Staff 1983

Back row: Mrs Underwood, Mrs Badnell, Mrs Heffer (secretary), Mrs Trainor,
Mrs Million, Mrs Doughty, Mrs Fieldhouse, Mrs Packman
Front row: Mrs Choules, Mrs Harris, Mrs Arch, Mr Pitson, Mrs Edwards,
Mrs Morgan, Mrs Kendal

Staff 1992

Back row: Mrs Brown, Mr Butler, Mrs Crawshaw, Mrs Harris, Mrs Pound, Mrs Doughty,
Mrs Stowell, Mrs Bean, Mrs Tyldesley, Mrs Gibbon
Front row: Miss Woodruff, Mrs Pelling, Mrs Kendal, Mrs Merricks, Mr Pitson,
Mrs Bickerton, Mrs Choules, Mrs Hutchinson, Mrs Abbey

Technology

The first computers in classrooms were primitive by today's standards. The program was loaded via a tape cassette player and the loading took about 20 minutes. So, to play a simple game, the computer was 'booted' and the 'play' button pressed on the cassette player. Then everyone had to do something else and then, on a good day, the program could be used. Eventually, the move was made to floppy disks which were about six inches square and which proved a bit more efficient. It was some years before every classroom had its own computer and the idea of a suite of computers was only a dream.

Youngsters key in to computers

SONNING Common Primary School is one of seven schools in Oxfordshire to be chosen by the county to take part in a pilot scheme to find out about the use of computers in primary schools.

Under the scheme the school received a £700 computer free in the first week of this term.

At present, both staff and children are learning how to operate their new piece of equipment. Mrs Jill Kendal, who teaches a third and fourth year class at the school, has been on a computer course and she is teaching the rest of the teachers.

Sonning Common's new headmaster, Mr Stuart Pitson, the former deputy head, said: "At the moment we are experimenting to find out just what we can do with it and, how we can use it. In about 12 or 18 months' time we shall have to write a report for the county on our experiences.

"So far all the juniors have had an opportunity to do something with it, even if it's only been to get used to the keyboard.

The fourth year children have done quite a lot and we've made a tape with them.

"In one class which has been involved, the teacher has been taking groups of four children for half an hour the end of that time the children are quite confident.

"I've been told it takes a child 30 minutes to get u a computer and and adult three hours.

"After Christmas we asked the children how ma them had had computers or electronic toys for Chri and we found over two thirds of them had had some k electronic gadget.

"We'd be daft to do anything other than develop interest in school, if we don't we shall be way behir children."

As well as learning to use their computer, the pu Sonning Common are currently writing about their e ences with the computer and a display of computer w to be put up in the school for parents to see when collect and deliver their children.

Next term Mr Pitson hopes to have a parents' even show them the way the school is using the compute involve them in some of the work.

He said: "We have a number of dads who are i computing business who have offered to help.

Despite the interest in new technology at So Common all the usual activities are continuing.

Film shows are held regularly after school fo children. On Monday they saw "Greyfriars Bobby' earlier in the term they watched "The Great M Caper." After half term "The Love Bug' is to be shc

On March 4 the PTA are holding a beetle driv parents and children in the shcool hall. This is a popular event at the school and tickets are usually sol several days in advance.

The PTA are also planning to hold a food auctio March 18 when jars, bottles and tins will be sold to money for school funds.

Mr Pitson said: "Any spare money is being sav replace our minibus.

Henley Standard 1983

In 1987 Mrs Kendal's class used 'cutting edge' technology to undertake a project about the school. This is the result, part of a school handbook for new pupils.

```
    Sonning Common Primary School


The School has 350 pupils, it is  now mu
ch smaller than it was a few years ago.
The children start at 5 and go on until
11. Then they transfer to the Comprehens
ive  -Chiltern Edge, which is also in th
e village.
   The primary school has extensive playin
g fields and many nice trees and  a wild
area. There is a pond and green houses s
o lots of outdoor work from the environm
ent can be done.
About half stay to school dinners, most
of the rest have packed lunch.
A lot of the children do wear school uni
form of blue and grey, though it is not
compulsory.
```

Computers for the school office were even further behind. A log book entry in September 1989 reads: Demonstration of electric typewriter for Mrs Heffer, school secretary. In 1991 an office computer was installed for the first time and Mrs Pam Gibbon became the school secretary and bursar.

1987 - problem solving in Mrs Bean's class

Children in the junior school produced topic books in the junior years. This poem is an extract from Catherine Rockell's 1992 Rainforest Project.

A POEM . --- GUESS WHAT I AM?

I am standing hear dreading
what could happen any minute.
All of a sudden I might be chopped down.
And made into paper or used as firewood.
This may not happen if I have someone caring for me.
So just think how many trees are getting chopped down every time
you use a piece of paper.
Just a bit of effort that is all it needs.

by Catherine Rockell.

guessed what I was? -- A TREE.

Guide Dogs for the Blind

Over many years the school had a close connection with Guide Dogs for the Blind and class trips to their Wokingham Centre were frequent. The foyer was decorated in the 1980s with many photographs of dogs whose training had been paid for by donations from the school (in 1986 for example, £400 was donated). Silver foil was collected for many years as were bottle tops from the infants' daily third pint bottles. When Mr Pitson retired, the last dog sponsored by the school was named 'Stuart' in his honour. Mrs Badnell and Mrs Webb (a parent) were particularly involved with Guide Dogs and when Mrs Badnell left the school in 1989 she donated a trophy with a guide dog standing on it which has been awarded every year since then to a pupil who has demonstrated outstanding service to the school and community. The winners are listed in Appendix 3.

School trips and visits

Pupils continued to enjoy residential and day trips all over the country and further afield. The Peak District, the Isle of Wight, Swanage, the Wye Valley, Shrewsbury, Winterbourne Abbotts, Tregoyd, Hampton Court, the Forest of Dean, Capel-y-Ffin and the Dolomites were all visited and in 1988 the school football team travelled to Florida to play against American sides for 2 weeks. An extended trip for Mrs Kendal in 1987 saw her swapping roles with American teacher Mrs Pauline Levin from New York for two terms.

1986 trip to Isle of Wight

Local trips were also enjoyed –

Mrs Badnell's class in 1987 finding out how British Rail worked.

Parents

Ever since its inception, the PTA has supported the school and raised many thousands of pounds at Summer and Christmas Fetes. This money has been used for many projects over the years including providing the school with a minibus for residential and local trips.

Anna and Sally Irwin entering the fancy dress competition in 1990

1990 Mrs Irwin and Mrs Pilcher 'manning' the plant stall

A good fund raiser in 1992

Tudor Celebrations

In 1987 the school held a series of events on a Tudor theme. The entire school went on a trip to Hampton Court which was very successful and the first time everyone had gone out for a day together.

In June there was a celebration on the playground with Tudor dancing and Tudor songs. Everyone dressed for the occasion. Mr Pitson wrote-

> *'Parents and members of the public came to school to see a demonstration of Tudor games on the field. Tudor herbs, posies and wares were sold. There was a grand parade from the field onto the playground where the children performed Tudor dances and songs to the accompaniment of the school orchestra. Visitors were then shown around the classrooms to see Tudor displays.'*

The Tudor Parade

Back row: Mr Pitson, Mrs Wilkinson, Mrs Brown, Mrs Fieldhouse, Mrs Levin, Mrs Badnell, Mrs Thompson, Mrs Bain, Mrs Heffer
Front row: Mrs Choules, Mrs Abbey, Mrs Twyman, Mrs Edwards (as one of Henry V111's wives), Mr Edwards (Henry V111), Mrs Bean

The school was asked to perform the dances and songs at the Herb Farm in Sonning Common and at Greys Court near Henley as that is a Tudor building.

Mr Edwards and Mr Pitson at Greys Court in their Tudor costumes

Art

Under the guidance of Mrs Twyman, amongst many other talented artists, the school produced wonderful displays of art work for the school and community.

Giant Christmas cards in Victorian style by Dean Owen, Neil Hughes, ?, Luke Daniels and Carol Pickett

1984 – Mrs Choules class – The Nativity - Clare West, Claire Dean, Kelly Myhill, Matthew Allum, Matthew Ashley and Peter Mills

Music and Drama

The musical talents of Mrs Arch and Mrs Bean and the dramatic direction of Mrs Kendal amongst others ensured that this was a period when children were involved annually in fabulous shows. These included 'Queen Beryl and the Romans', 'Baboushka', 'Mighty Mississippi', 'The Evacuees' (a particular favourite), 'Swinging Samson', 'The Angry Arrow', 'Will Wanderers Win', 'The Wizard of Wazz', 'Blast – Off', 'David and Goliath', 'The Golden Legend,' 'Pied Piper of Hamelin', 'Joseph' and in 1991 'Yanomamo' produced by Mrs Kendal and which Mr Pitson described (and anyone who remembers it will agree) as the best he had ever seen. At that show alone, £460 was raised and many hundreds of pounds more from other shows which went either to charities or to buy theatrical lights or other equipment for future productions.

The Christmas tradition of staff performing for the children began towards the end of this period – who could forget Mr Edwards appearing in Beardilocks and the Bears!

Health and Safety

There were no major health issues during this period though an outbreak of hepatitis affecting 9 children caused a bit of a stir in 1990. The big issue as ever was nits – how to avoid them, how to get rid of them and whose fault was it. Although everyone was concerned, when a meeting was held in 1987 with a film and advice from the school nurse, only 7 parents turned up. Mr Pitson tried again in 1990 and this time 2 parents turned up.

The weather was more disruptive to the smooth running of the school. The outside toilets froze and could not be used during the winters of 1986, 1987 and 1991 as snow lay on the ground but the school remained open. In 1989 there was even snow in April providing what Mr Pitson described as *'winter in the summer term'*.

During the storm of 1987 the polythene greenhouse ripped, the flat roof over the paper store leaked, an apple tree was blown down in the Dobinson Paddock and many branches came down –but still the school remained open. However, in January 1990 gale force winds meant the school had no electricity from 10a.m. and all roads to Sonning Common were blocked by fallen trees. The last child was not collected from school until 5.10p.m. There was no electricity for 3 days so a closure was forced.

Links with Bishopswood School

The school's link with Bishopswood Special School began modestly under the headship of Mr Sharman and blossomed during Mr Pitson's period as head. The two schools were determined to encourage the integration of pupils from both schools to their mutual benefit. Two classes of pupils from Bishopswood's main building in Horspond Road had moved into Sonning Common classrooms and everyone joined together for a wide variety of social and educational experiences. Playtimes, assemblies, mealtimes, concerts and school trips were often shared. National and international media interest was shown and visitors from all over this country and further afield visited to see integration in action. Both the Times Educational Supplement and the BBC ran features on the scheme. Oxfordshire granted the school additional staffing (Mrs Hutchinson) to enhance opportunities for children from both schools to work alongside each other. In 1985, the first joint Christmas concert was organised by Mrs Gould (Bishopswood class teacher) and Mrs Choules and in 1988, Mrs Choules was seconded to the staff of Bishopswood School for 2 years. Opportunities were sought for the pupils to share activities equally. One such activity was a sponsored brick build in 1988 which was very successful with proceeds shared between the two schools. Children simply built a tower of play bricks as high as they could before it toppled. This was an activity where all could participate on equal terms.

Pupils from Sonning Common and Bishopswood working together and helping each other

Sport

Sport continued to play a very important part in school life. Sports Days continued to be held annually and in 1991 the school added 2 new 'houses' to the competition so that pupils were now grouped in Tudor, Windsor, Stuart and Hanover houses.

Football and netball were the main team sports and rivalry between Sonning Common and other local schools was as keen as ever.

Football 1984

Back row: Steven Butterfield, Toby Pullen, Matthew Hayward, Richard Stammers, Stuart Elder
Front row: Mark Treadwell, Julian Lambden, Russell Pickett, Stuart Stone, Gareth Handley

The Morrell Shield was an Oxfordshire Competition that had been contested at least since the 1950s and the successful team below won it in 1988. They were not the first or last Sonning Common Team to do so.

Football 1988

Back row: Mark Morris, Christopher James, Gareth Britton, Krister Jones, Edward Curzon,
Middle row: Mr Edwards, Andrew Howells, Warren Clayton, Greg Tyldesley, Peter Mills, David Lowe
Front row: David Watkins, Andrew Leaver, Matthew Stowell, Adam Girdler, David Pickett

1983
netball
team

Back row: Clare Borland, Michelle Hughes, Samantha Chevis, Lisa
Front row: Katherine Macleod, Sarah Cottrell, Jane Gardener, Linda Buckner,
Hilary Coote

1990
netball
team

Back row: Carly Readings, Amanda Watkins, Mrs Tyldesley, Donna Clark,
Karen Williams,
Front row: Yvette Hancock, Marieke Tyldesley (now Mrs Fox) Natasha Sloan,
Rosalinda Jones

A large school like Sonning Common was able to field more than one team for each sport.

In 1986 Mr Edwards took the cricket team to The Oval where they lost every game but nobody minded.

In 1990 Mr Edwards was granted a year's unpaid leave to work in America and never returned. Mrs Bean took on the role of acting deputy head but poor health prevented her from taking the job permanently.

In April 1992 Mrs Choules replaced Mrs Bean as deputy head. Unexpectedly, in June 1992 Mr Pitson told startled staff that he would be taking early retirement and finishing at the end of term. Mr Pitson and Mrs Bean signed off with a performance of Joseph and were presented with giant cards and gifts. There was no time for a successor to be found by September so Mrs Choules having only been deputy for a few months was caterpaulted into acting headship, the only woman ever to have the role.

Clive Mills (chair of Governors) and Mrs Choules (right) say farewell to Mrs Diana Bean and Mr Stuart Pitson

<h1>Chapter Eleven</h1>
<h2>The 75th Anniversary 1988</h2>

*I*n January 1988 Mr Pitson wrote:

'On January 6th the school was 75 years old. It opened as an all age school in 1913. We are hoping to celebrate, but in the summer term when the weather is kinder. During the week commencing June 13th we are planning all kinds of celebrations.'

Staff 1988

Back row: Mrs S Karavis, Mrs M. Choules, Mrs C. Parry, Mrs D. Hoyle, Mrs P. Doughty, Mrs C. Thompson, Mr P. Bean
Middle row: Mrs D. Bean, Mrs S. Tyldesley, Mrs P. Twyman, Mrs R. Brown, Mrs P. Elvish, Mrs A. Disney, Mrs J. Hutchinson, Mrs S. Badnell, Mrs S. Heffer
Front row: Mrs J. Bain, Mrs C. Davies, Mrs M. Fieldhouse, Mr S. Pitson, Mr S. Edwards, Mrs C. Abbey, Mrs J. Kendal

Events took place throughout the year. Mr Pitson took children to interview former pupils including Mr Wheatley (aged 83) who was at the school when it opened in 1913, Mr Dolphin, Mr Wright who attended in 1925 and Mrs Holmes (aged 78).

The main week of celebrations took place in June. This is the programme of events.

13th June – An evening of Nostalgia – slides from 1957 onwards

14th June – School open until 9 p.m. for people to see the exhibition of classroom displays and photographs

15th June – Pageant - school open until 9 p.m. for people to see the exhibition

16th June – School open until 9 p.m. for people to see the exhibition

17th June – Old Time Music hall

18th June – Village Day fete

All week – Display of children's art in the Village Hall

Claire Manning designed a cover for the Village magazine

The pageant featured all the children in the school and the Bishopswood classes too. Every class chose a decade and produced a cameo of music and dance based on that period.

A 1920s flapper

1913 - 1920

Depicting the early years of the school

Katy Sunman and Mrs Choules dressed for the 1940s

Mr Edwards class took the 1960s as their decade

Cause for jubilation

A silver jubilee of a King and Queen was among features of a pageant given by pupils of Sonning Common Primary School on Wednesday to mark the school's 75th anniversary and here George V (Ian Elgy) and Mary (Rachel Soden) step out 1935-style to the strains of "The Lambeth Walk" and "You Must Have Been A Beautiful Baby" followed by Mallard steam train driver (James Saoulis) and housemaid (Tracey Smith). See more pictures and stories on pages 16 and 17.

Henley Standard

Pageant spanning 75 glorious years

A grand pageant depicting life and events over the past three-quarters of a century took place at Sonning Common Primary School on Wednesday.

It was a glorious celebration of the school's 75th anniversary from its beginnings in 1913 until today. Some 500 people, including former staff and pupils, some of whom had travelled long distances for the occasion, attended the festivities.

Over the past months, each class has been studying the historical events and learning some of the songs and dances of one particular decade in the school's existence and notable incidents which took place in the world during those years were depicted in song, dance and mime by the children, all wearing the clothes from that period.

From the suffragettes, wounded soldiers and VAD's of the Great War, to Mickey Mouse, Chicago gangsters and flappers of the Roaring Twenties, the pageant progressed through to the Thirties with Pearly Kings and Queens, Edward VIII and Mrs. Simpson and the Jarrow marchers.

Servicemen, evacuees and Land girls were all there from the 1940's and Teddy Boys and girls with flared skirts and wasp belts evoked fond memories of the Fifties. The Swinging Sixties were portrayed with Flower Power and the assassination of President Kennedy as well as some of the many other events of that decade.

The 1970's and 1980's were covered by the three infant classes, among whom were such notable characters as Kermit the Frog, Miss Piggy and the Mr. Men.

As well as acting out short sketches to depict the various incidents, the children also performed songs and dances from each decade, including the Gay Gordons, Twist, Hokey Cokey, Lambeth Walk, Charleston and Jive.

It was an afternoon of nostalgia for many, particularly those who attended the school in its very early days. Afterwards, a group of former teachers told the *Standard* how much they had all enjoyed the afternoon.

"It was thoroughly delightful", said Mrs. Betty Dawson who had travelled from Dorset. And Mrs. Jean Welch, also a former teacher who now lives near Bridport, summed it all up by saying: "It was the same excellent standard that one comes to expect from this school."

Deputy head, Steve Edwards as a Hippie. His class represented the Sixties and sang the Beatles 'What would you do . .', currently at No. 1 for Wet Wet Wet. Margaret Fieldhouse led her class through the 20's, dancing the Charleston and singing songs from 'The Boyfriend'.

Henley Standard

Mr Pitson recorded the events of the week in the school log book:

'Monday evening's slide show was packed out with parents, ex-pupils, and members of the local community. Everyone seemed to enjoy themselves as they 'wallowed in nostalgia.' The evening did not finish until 10 p.m. On Tuesday evening the school was open until 9 o'clock and many people came to see the classroom displays and the photographic exhibition, which had photographs from 1913 to the present day.

Wednesday was the day of the Pageant. It was very hot and sunny, a change from the inclement weather of the rest of the summer. Three hundred chairs were put out for our visitors, all were filled and people stood 5 to 6 deep behind them. The children told the history from 1913 to the present day in music and dance and the history of the school was included in this. Everyone performed beautifully and thanks must be recorded to all the staff for their hard work and for the parents and friends who produced such superb costumes.

Two ex- headteachers, Mr Miller and Mr Enever were among the many guests who attended the light refreshments in the school hall at the end of the afternoon. Mrs Ockenden and Mrs Wise from the canteen produced a feast rather than afternoon tea. Mrs Tyldesley, a member of staff, made a 75ᵗʰ Birthday Cake. The school was open until 9p.m. and again on Thursday evening.

On Friday evening, the PTA, staff and children performed an 'Old Time Music Hall' in the school hall. Most of the audience came in period costume and a superb evening's entertainment was enjoyed by everyone.

Saturday afternoon was the Village Day Fete, organised by the PTA and the Parish Council. Throughout the week, an Art Exhibition was held in the Village Hall. This was organised by Mrs Twyman and included children's work from over 20 years ago.

The school bell was rung every morning at 8.50 a.m. as used to happen, in previous years. On Friday morning Mrs Howell (pupil in 1913) fulfilled a lifelong ambition and rang the bell.

The whole idea of the 75th celebrations, in my mind, was to bring the village community together and looking back at the end of the week it certainly seems as though we succeeded.

As far as I am concerned, the whole week of celebrations surpassed my wildest dreams, as everyone in the village joined in the celebrations.'

Mrs Howell, with Matthew Stowell, rings the school bell

Chapter Twelve
Mr A P Marples 1993 – 2008

In September 1992 Mr Philip Marples was appointed the next headteacher. He was unable to leave his post as head of Badgemore School, Henley, until December and so began his tenure in January 1993. There were 248 children on roll in 10 classes, grouped vertically in 2 year age bands. By 2004 this had risen to 324 pupils. Owing to budget restraints, the way in which the children were divided into classes changed nearly every year and sometimes a particularly small year group led to an extra large class with additional support.

Back row: Mrs Gibbon, Mrs Pound, Mrs Harris, Mrs John, Mrs Evans, Mrs Merricks,   1993 staff
Mrs Doughty, Mrs Stowell, Mrs Tilbury
Front row: Mrs Brown, Miss Woodruff, Mrs Pelling, Mrs Choules, Mr Marples,
Mrs Kendal, Mrs Hughes, Mrs Thompson, Mrs Tyldesley

Alongside the National Curriculum, in 1995 the Government introduced SATs (Standard Attainment Tasks) for 11 year olds covering English, mathematics and science. The dilemma arose of whether to teach to the test (possibly reaping higher results) or keeping the broad and balanced curriculum which challenged pupils and which the school espoused. Mr Marples was concerned about *the validity of tests and the extent to which children feel pressurised*. He further commented:

> *'Target Setting is the name of the new game-improving schools by obtaining better test results. There is a view that better examination results mean better education. I don't subscribe to this view.'*

The Education (Schools) Act of 1992 introduced a national scheme of inspections known as the Office for Standards in Education (Ofsted). Her Majesty's inspectors would supervise the inspection of each state-funded school in the country, and would publish its reports instead of reporting to the Secretary of State.

The first Ofsted inspection took place between October 7th and 11th 1996 – a whole week plus a meeting with parents the previous week. A team of 7 inspectors looked into every aspect of school life. The outcome was a grading of 'satisfactory' though there was especial praise for I.T., French, music, extra-curricular activities, swimming and pupils' ability to express themselves. There was criticism of the presentation of pupils' work and the shortage of non-fiction books in the infant library. A second inspection took place in October 2000 and a third in November 2005. Each inspection was shorter and with fewer inspectors than the previous one as it was realised that an impossible task was faced with the huge number of schools waiting to be inspected.

Parents

Parental participation in all aspects of school life was a cornerstone of Mr Marples philosophy and within 3 weeks of taking up his post he was meeting with parents about a new school brochure and in 1999 the first Home/School Agreement was published.

The Parent Forum became a regular feature under Mr Marples, discussing homework, class organisation, bullying, healthy eating and school starting and finishing times to name but a few. Parents were able to introduce any topic they chose. As a result, a 'no crisps at playtime, only healthy snacks' policy was agreed and in 2004 a government inspired scheme encouraging '5 a day' meant free fruit daily for infants.

As a result of Parent Forums, the school reported all head injuries (however minor) directly to parents, a calendar for the year was distributed each September and all communications from school began to go out on Thursdays. Parents were consulted about changing the times of the school day in 1997 which resulted in a shorter lunch break and school finishing at 3.15p.m. Parental consultations were changed from evenings to be all day on the Friday before February half term with a creche available.

From 1993 an after-school club was introduced to support working parents and from 2002 a breakfast club was added.

One of many PTA events was the summer fete 1998, with a sporting theme for a world cup year.

Good sports at school fete day

The 26.1998

A SPORTING theme was the order of the day at Sonning Common Primary School summer fete last weekend.

With World Cup fever running high, 'beat the goalie' proved to be a popular attraction. Also high on the action list were demonstrations by members of the Sonning Common Cricket Club. "The children loved bowling against real cricketers," said PTA chairman Gail Kelly.

Around £3,300 was raised at the event which is destined to go towards providing better library facilities at the school.

Pictured left: 10-year-old Sean Mott from Sonning Common tries out his putting skills R 98.452.22

Pictured right: Geoffrey Maul, Keith Davis, Jeff Harris and Roger Choules from Sonning Common Cricket Club R 98 452 15

Henley Standard

The school tea towel was an excellent fundraiser again in 1995.

Curriculum

Mr Marples immediately introduced Curriculum Sharing evenings where teachers met the parents of their new class each September and presented a summary of the year's topics and themes. These continue today.

French for junior classes was innovative in its time but parents made a voluntary contribution to cover the cost in the first few years and French for Key Stage 1 (ages 5 – 7) came later. Subject weeks were held regularly and included English, thinking, science, maths, art, Africa, sport, music, food, design/technology, geography, health, protect our planet and book weeks. Children completed projects on different topics throughout Key Stage 2.

Extract from Thomas Rockell's 1998 Rainforest project

Visits from well known authors helped to encourage pupils with their reading and writing. In 1997, author Val Biro came along with his vintage car 'Gumdrop', about which he wrote many stories.

Sonning Common School had always had a good reputation for supporting less able pupils and in the 1990s strategies for more able pupils began to loom large – whole school topics such as 'how to stop a cat and a dog fighting' and 'what improvements would you make to the design of the human body' encouraged all pupils to get thinking but the most able to let their imagination run wild. In 2002 the first whole school debate was held with the question, 'Should children have TVs in their bedroom?' Following the speeches, the children voted by exiting the hall through the 'yes' or 'no' door. The result was a resounding success for 'yes' by 204 votes to 71. The next debate asked, 'Which makes the better pet, a cat or a dog?' The result is not recorded.

Two contributions from Mr Marples cannot go unmentioned – Values Education and the Comenius Project. Values based education was introduced in 1999 and worked to instil in pupils (and adults) the core values of Love, Peace, Truth, Right Conduct and Non-Violence. This continues in the school today albeit in a slightly different form.

John Amos Comenius, born 1592 in Moravia, believed in Universal Education and the project that bears his name encourages educators and children from different countries to connect in order to cement the feeling of togetherness. The school connection began in 2001 and over a number of years, teachers visited schools in France, Spain and Norway and everyone enjoyed their reciprocal visits to Sonning Common.

Extra- curricular clubs and activities

As well as the annual residential trips and day trips for younger children which have been a feature of the school since 1913, a wide range of activities was available for pupils to enjoy in their spare time. In June 1994 the first Year 5 camp was held with 44 children 'sleeping' under canvas in the paddock whilst 4 adults supervised games and a barbecue, followed by art work with Mrs Twyman.

Mr Marples was a musician and keen sportsman so it was unsurprising that as well as Mrs Tyldesley's football team, tag rugby, running, netball and even golf were available. In 1993, Mr Choules coached the Kwik Cricket club, which had 30 participants on its first meeting and 50 at its peak.

There was also a school orchestra which met before school and at lunchtime and the unforgettable hand chimes groups which performed on many occasions. Drum and percussion lessons were available and in 2004, talented musician Luke Daniels (a former pupil) taught groups from Year Two to play the penny whistle. There were also chess, pottery and art, horticultural and table tennis clubs.

Many will remember the wonderful firework displays organised by parents Vic and Jane Darnell. The first of these in 1994 was on the school field and by 1996 an audience of 1000+ attended. A victim of its own success, the display moved to Bishopswood sports ground in 1997 after complaints from a neighbour and amid safety fears.

ICT

The importance of ICT became increasingly great and in 1999, £36,000 was set aside to build and equip an ICT suite. In the middle of his summer break, Mr Marples arrived to see the start of the project. Unfortunately, all did not go to plan:

> '18th August 1999 – official commencement date for building alterations to the computer room next to the Old Hall. No one came and no one knew where anyone was!'

The first school website appeared in 1999 and in 2002 the school bought its first trolley of laptop computers. In 2003, amid much excitement, the first interactive whiteboard was installed.

Premises

A great many changes to the premises took place during Mr Marples time as headteacher, the most major being the demolition of the HORSA buildings which had been in place since 1946. The first went in August 2000 to make way for the Bishopswood building which opened in 2002 and the second, which had housed the old dining hall was demolished on 19th February 2003. Also in 2000 the much loved and hated outside toilet block was finally removed. These 'facilities' had still been in use as late as March 1995 when Mr Marples reported that the outdoor walls were to be repointed.

The infant playground area in the late 1990s had no special area for younger children and the HORSAs can still be seen in the background. The Lea Road entrance at the same time had no safety path built in.

In 2002 the official opening of the new Bishopswood School took place with the building named after Valerie Northfield who was headteacher at the time.

When the old dining hall was demolished, Year 6 moved temporarily into the old library building but were into the 'East wing' in September 2003 with the official opening on September 26th. The sub-soil from this build was used to create the amphitheatre in the Dobinson Paddock and in 2004, forty parents and children spent a very wet Saturday completing the seating.

Amphitheatre

When Bishopswood School moved to their new building, a decision was made to establish an Early Years Unit (EYU) in the classrooms they had occupied and in September 2003 the Kites unit opened with Miss Bartlett in charge. The Playgroup provided 'wraparound' care in the adjacent classroom so that children could stay at school all day. The official opening with a real red kite and a balloon launch was in November.

From 2002 there was discussion of plans to redevelop the main entrance, Headteacher's office, administrative and medical areas. This finally happened in 2007 but as you can see from the picture below all was not completed in time for the start of term. Luckily, the weather was clement.

Before

During

Other notable events during these years include the erection of the trim trail in 1997 designed by Mr Marples and Mrs Tyldesley and built by parent Cliff Readings. The PTA provided £4,500 for the project and in 2001 the Willow Classroom was planted and used as an outside shady space.

Trim Trail

Willow Classroom

School and Community

Mr Marples saw the school very much as part of the wider community and was delighted when the village library was relocated to the old hall area where it had been housed many years earlier. This was first mentioned as a possibility in March 1999 and the decision to go ahead made in December of that year. There were initial concerns over pupil safety which needed to be resolved. On completion, Mr Marples wrote:

'The library looks stunning in all its primary colours glory.'

The official opening by Councillor David Green took place on November 13th 2000 with balloons, ribbons and presentations. In 2002 Mrs Brewer left and in 2003 Mrs Rosemary Dunstan became the new librarian for the school and the village.

2001 – an event in the new library

2006 - a visit from illustrator and author Korky Paul

When the Sonning Common Lunch Club faced the possibility of having to disband Mr Marples was instrumental in arranging their new venue at the school.

What a difference a year makes!

Cheers! Pensioners raise a toast to 25 years of the Sonning Common Lunch Club — an anniversary it looked likely they would not reach.

Towards the end of last year the club was faced with the prospect of singing for its last supper when Oxfordshire County Council adult learning classes were given priority use of the rooms they used.

However, thanks to Philip Marples, head teacher at Sonning Common Primary School, which owns the old library building in Grove Road, the club now has a new venue for its monthly meetings which are run on a voluntary basis by Freda Buckner and six other ladies, on the second Wednesday of every month.

At the first lunch in the new venue last week, members raised a toast to a happier future.

060167

Henley Standard

Sport

Throughout its history, Sonning Common has been a school where sport is played for competition and for fun. Sports Day has always been a day for individuals to shine but also for teamwork and encouragement for the less sporty. From 1997, the infant sports have been held in the morning and junior sports in the afternoon – and from 1998 in the Paddock instead of the main field.

In 2002 Mr Marples opened the school at 7.30am so that children could see England play Nigeria in the football world cup. Eighty five came with another 90 at half time. He did it again for England v Brazil with the PTA serving biscuits and juice at half time.

This team from 1995 won the Morrell Shield.

Shield win for young footballers

Teacher and coach Sue Tyldesley with the winning team.

Back row: Matthew Gould, James Morley, Adam Huggins, Jonathan McGill, Mrs Tyldesley, Philip Wise, Robert Singer, Nicholas Blodwell
Front row: Ben Bailey, Steven Braisher, Guy Bickerton, Adam Stowell, Edward Bickerton, Robbie Rix

There have been many, many teams over the years but here are a few of them.

Football 1998

Back row: Thomas Jardine, Jonathan Moss, Tom Pinder, Thomas Fiander, Matthew Newton, Joe Trimby, George Brewer
Front row: Charlie Kew, Thomas Rockell, Andrew Hawkins, James Betts, Harry Pells

Netball 2000

Back row: Emma Samways, Francesca Taylor, Emily Duckworth, Laura Neighbour, Alice Cummins
Front row: James Smith, Louise Butler-Smith, Liam Taylor, Karen Davies, Fergus Adamson

In 2004 the team won the South Oxfordshire U11 tag rugby competition. The headteacher was very proud and commented: '*Kirsty Boyd scored the most determined solo try I have ever seen*'.

2004 Tag Rugby Team

Back row: Matthew Thomas, Robert Miller, Sian Ralph, Kirsty Boyd, Taylor Vines, Tom Green
Front row: Ellie Kirby, Ben Conway, Kristian Parsons, Sam Hargreaves, Christian White, Thomas Kelly, Elody Fumi

Back row: Markland Tidswell, Emily Estcourt, Tom Mee, Maisie Stevens, Matthew Slater, Luke Pitson
Front row: Michael Barker, Daniel Slater, Chelsea Hartman, Emma Dawson

This successful cricket team from 2008 won a Kwik Cricket competition at Kidmore End School.

Plays and Musicals

The staff has a tradition of 'performing' for the children at the last assembly before Christmas usually producing something at the last moment which is associated with whatever is popular at the time. These have included Snow White and the 9 Dwarves, the Teletubbies, Bob the Builder, the Grumpy Innkeeper, the England rugby world cup win, Ali Baba and Strictly Come Dancing. Special mention must be made of the 2002 effort which saw Mr Marples as Will Young, Mr McIntosh as Gareth Gates and Mr Harmer as Darius in Pop Idol. This led to unprecedented scenes of children queuing at the staff room at playtime to ask for their autographs!

Year 6 and other classes have entertained their parents, peers and parents over the years with Kalasia (rather spoilt for Mr Marples by *one child chewing gum*'), The Evacuees, Sago the Clown, Blast-off, Tadpole Rag and Caterpillar Boogie, The Pyramid, The Dream-Catcher, The Adventures of Bobo Peep and Peter Pan.

Sago the Clown 1997

In July 1994, pupils, staff and parents joined together for an Old Time Music Hall which Mr Marples described as:

> *'A wonderful example of children, parents and staff working superbly together.'*

Members of the community were invited to celebrate Harvest Festival with the children and share the produce from their display.

Young and old unite to celebrate Harvest Festival

Henley Standard

In addition, there was always a play or concert at Christmas time including in 1995 the first outdoor concert with the Salvation Army Band and a real donkey.

Hundreds join in the dancing

A tableau from Sonning Common's Dance Nativity.

A Dance Nativity involving almost 290 children was the ambitious Christmas production at Sonning Common Primary School.

Every child took part in the show which told the story of the Christmas story in a number of dances.

Each class performed several dances illustrating a particular theme. These included a Mary and Joseph dance, soldiers' and shepherds' dances, and an oriental and a Silent Night dance.

There were some musical interludes and the nativity story, which had been written in verse by the children, were read by them in between each dance.

This is the first time that the whol school has performed together in on production. Four shows were given to parents this week and a selection o dances was also performed at Caver sham Methodist Church.

Christmas 1994   Henley Standard

Health and Safety

Traffic problems had occurred in Grove Road ever since the school opened in 1913 and arose again when a 4 year old was knocked over by a car though not badly hurt. Mr Marples tried to take action to prevent a repeat but Oxfordshire road engineering department considered Grove Road a 'low risk' and would not put in yellow lines. School experience over many years suggested a much higher risk.

In 1994, the use of seat belts in the school minibus and on coach trips became a big issue following a series of accidents nationally. Some parents would not allow their children to travel without one and, later that year, belts were fitted to the school minibus. Seatbelts on coaches followed some time later and there was a period when a few parents preferred to take their own children to a venue rather than allowing them to travel without a belt.

Increased concern was also shown by parents about pupil safety on residential trips. This lead to a decision not to use youth hostels where secondary age groups might be sharing the accommodation. Pupil safety was always a priority on any trip and teachers were always prepared to be woken by any child experiencing a problem but a line was drawn when a parent suggested that a teacher should 'stay awake all night' and sit 'on guard'. The usual problem on residential trips is persuading the children to sleep at all.

Following the terrible events at Dunblane Primary School (March 1996) an urgent meeting of governors was held to discuss school security, safety and coping with crises. In October 1996 the school was broken into – at that time there was no alarm system. In 1998 staff were issued with name badges, police checks for parent helpers were introduced and staff challenged unauthorised adults in and around the buildings. New gates and fences were erected and in 2007 the first cctv cameras were installed.

Sometimes, safety issues have been caused by pupils. There was a tradition of carol singing around the village at Christmas time until one year as Mr Marples noted:

> *'Four children disappeared during the trek around the neighbourhood. However – they turned up at the end when we returned having spent the time at a friend's house across the road from school – severely punished by parents and school!'*

In 1997 a pupil rang 999 whilst the orchestra were playing at Oxford Youth Prom. The fire service turned up and almost evacuated the whole building. The child's parents were asked to take *'very stern measures'*.

Major health scares have become very uncommon although head lice seem to be a problem that never goes away. In 2000, all the children were immunised against meningitis which *'caused quite an upset'*. The next day 10 children were absent due to bad reaction to the injection - *'This was reported to the medical services who replied that we obviously had a bad batch of vaccine!'*

School trips

Mr Marples encouraged staff and pupils to engage in residential visits and joined in himself when he could. He was famously the chief cook when groups went to Hill End, near Farmoor in Oxfordshire. Staff sometimes felt that he was enjoying himself so much he forgot there were children to be closely supervised. This cartoon given to him by Joseph Fuller in 1998 suggests that perhaps the children agreed.

The Millennium

The school celebrated the millennium with a Cobble Garden and a time capsule. The Cobble Garden, under the guidance of teacher Mrs Mills, was made up of a series of large cobbles in six segments, decorated by every child and every adult connected with the school. With a limited colour palette these were all unique and looked beautiful. Andy Parry and Dave Burling did the digging and set the cobbles in place. Unfortunately, the 'weatherproof' paint proved not to be and disappointingly quickly the paint began to flake and eventually had to be removed, leaving plain stones which nevertheless still look impressive. The contents of the time capsule will be revealed at a date in the future.

The Millennium cobble garden.

R:00.0704.14

Henley Standard

Back row: Mrs Hanks, Mrs Merricks, Mrs Stowell, Mrs Matthews, Mrs Doughty   Staff 2000
Middle row: Mrs Tyldesley, Mrs Harris, student, Mrs Brightling, Mrs Hems,
Miss Mantle, Mrs Gibbon
Front row: Mrs Pound, Mrs Mills, Mrs Willis, Miss Craig, Mr Marples,
Mrs Choules, Miss Bennett, Mrs Green, Mrs Willson

Bach row: Mrs McGowan, student, Mrs Genneper, Mr Feary, Mrs Merricks,   Staff 2008
Mrs Hinks, Mrs Stevenson
Middle row: Mrs Hems, Mrs Harris, Mrs Thurlow, Miss Price, Miss Offer,
Miss Carter, Mrs Hughes, Mrs Challis, Mrs Green
Front row: Mrs Hanks, Mrs Mills, Mrs Tyldesley, Mr Marples, Mrs White,
Mrs Matthews, Mr Lovegrove

Mr Marples wrote these words in July 2012, reflecting on his years at the school:

> '*My years at Sonning Common Primary School were set against the backdrop of many significant changes in education. Schools became used to managing their own budgets and became their own businesses. They produced their own development plans for learning, site management, and staff professional development, as the influence of the local authority waned. School inspections, which have become ever more draconian, led to many schools reducing the breadth of their curricula and often teaching to tests. Central government increasingly intruded into the classroom with initiatives such as literacy and numeracy which forever change because politicians and civil servants have no understanding of the true nature of learning.*
>
> *As head teacher of Sonning Common Primary School, therefore, it was important for me to establish that the staff, governors and I did our best to ensure the primacy of children's needs and mitigate the worst effects of a powerful yet ignorant central government and a diminishing local authority obedient to policies from Westminster. I feel the staff had considerable success with this in the way learning was developed for children with special needs, and with a varied and exciting curriculum for all.*

I wanted to give staff opportunities to demonstrate their talents and skills whilst working alongside children. We had expertise and enthusiasm at Sonning Common and the school was particularly rich in art, sport, music and environmental education.

I was also keen for the school to play an important part in village life. Including the library within the school walls was a major factor. Over the years, however, much success came from contributions made by parents, governors and villagers. The values the staff wove in to the curriculum established the school as a real and caring community and made a favourable impression in Sonning Common, with newspaper articles and a television item about them.

I was very happy as head teacher of Sonning Common Primary School, for the most part. As with all institutions, there were difficulties and problems. It was the unnecessary intrusions of government which led me to decide to retire early, as I found that I could no longer tread the tightrope of putting the children first and meeting the requirements of the current educational climate.

I want to thank all those wonderful people who made up the staff of our school, the children, parents, governors and members of the local community who contributed to a thriving and successful school.'

Mr Marples took the decision to retire in 2008 and left at Christmas. A fitting tribute was paid to him by staff and friends at an evening party which ended with a firework display.

Chapter Thirteen
A Teacher's story – Melanie White

*A*t Henley Grammar School in 1965 (the last cohort of pupils to take the 11+ examination in Oxfordshire) I had friends who had been at Sonning Common Primary School. I knew it was a much bigger school than the one I had attended and they all seemed to be good at sport and had already started learning French. Although I rode my bicycle to Sonning Common quite often, I had never seen the school buildings as they were tucked away in a side road and there was no reason for me to cycle along Grove Road.

When I completed my teacher training in 1975 I responded to an advert in the Henley Standard for a class teacher at the school and was successful in my application. So Miss Mills joined the staff in September 1975. This was recorded in the Manager's minutes. The staffing sub-committee recommended the appointment of a new member of staff :

> *'Miss M Mills, a young teacher on probation who successfully completed her training at King Alfred's college, Winchester. There are indications that this appointment will prove to be of benefit to our school.'*

Mr Johnson was the headmaster. It was still a very big school with 7 classes in the infants. I was given a class of 5 and 6 year olds whilst Miss Nesta Evans and Mrs Val Evans had the older infants next door with a moveable partition between the two rooms. Miss Evans was definitely 'old' school and pretty fearsome. I could hear the children next door doing everything in unison and her voice saying, *'Everyone start cutting now!'* and the snip, snip of scissors to follow. She had already been at the school for 31 years, had trained many years before, had risen to Head of the Infant Department and was one of two Deputy Heads of the school. Miss Evans had a guinea pig called Pepys which she would wheel around the department in a toy pram after all the children had departed. Mrs Val Evans was altogether more gentle. I never heard her raise her voice and she was simply disappointed if anyone misbehaved. My other colleagues in the infants were Mrs Aileen Edwards, Mrs Val Heywood, Mrs Janet Wilkes, Mrs Jean Welch, Mrs Judith Dodd and Mrs Cyndy Abbey.

This is a picture of one of my first classes, sent to me by Katharine Price who is third from the left in the front row. I remember also David Mills, John Palmer, Rachel Long, Toby Cole, Nigel Metcalf, Neil Halstead, Alastair Jenkinson, Kathryn Meheux, Sarah Cottrell and Erica Scrase.

The junior department of the school was more or less a completely separate school and we only met at the half -termly staff meeting which was a time for listening to Mr Johnson and nothing else. Mr Johnson was as frightening a character to me as he was for many pupils. He never called me anything but Miss Mills and to this day, I do not know what his initials RB stood for, though he was universally known as Johnny. He summoned me to his office one afternoon and I was as nervous as I would have been at 11 years old. My misdemeanour – I wrote up my register with boys and girls names mixed, as any modern young teacher would, but the strict rule here was boys first, then girls.

In 1977, Mr Johnson retired and was replaced by Mr Rod Sharman who was as different to Johnny as it was possible to be except in the respect that both liked to have their own way. The staff always believed that if Rod was wearing his red jumper they needed to watch out. Miss Mills became Mrs Choules in the summer holiday of 1977. The number of pupils on roll was falling quickly at this time and as the 'last one in' I always felt vulnerable to redeployment – I had no idea at that time how hard subsequent heads fought to retain their staff. Any thought of moving on to another school was overtaken by trying to keep any post at all. Rod worked to make the school more united and the formality of compulsory school uniform disappeared along with the keeping of parents at arm's length. Young teachers like myself perhaps found it easier to adapt to new ideas as I had trained recently and preferred to teach what was called 'The Integrated Day' which meant that not all pupils studied maths or English at the same time and which enabled the teacher to work with small groups. Presentation and display of children's work took on greater importance as did ongoing training for staff.

In 1983 Stuart Pitson became the next headteacher. Stuart led a settled period, consolidating the successful elements of Rod and Johnny's periods in charge. The wider curriculum encompassing sport, music, drama and school trips were important and the staff at this time were very capable of delivering in all these areas as well as the core subjects of English, maths and science. Stuart encouraged staff to develop their careers by taking external courses and I was fortunate to be granted a year's secondment to pursue a course at Oxford Polytechnic covering multiple aspects of education but particularly cementing my interest in children with special needs. On my return, I worked with Bishopswood school colleagues and in 1988 was seconded for a second time to become a member of staff at Bishopswood School for 2 years.

Having no particular training for this post was quite nerve wracking at first and would not have been possible without the wonderful support of my teaching assistant, Ruth Butler who, in truth, knew far more about it than I did. I discovered that I really enjoyed the challenge of teaching children with, in many cases, multiple difficulties and I learned that they needed support and help in much the same way as any child.

My first Bishopswood class was Adam Sinclair and David Walker at the back and, in front, Toby Heskins, Emily Watmough, Lisa Wilmer and Ellie Miles.

TEMPEST

During this period, however, came the worst moment of my career, ever! One of the children, an able boy with Down's Syndrome, took himself off to the toilet and did not return to the classroom. I went to see what he was up to and found he was not in the toilet or the corridor. Mr Pitson came to help and the school was searched from top to bottom. There was no sign of him and we discovered that his coat and bag had gone from the cloakroom too. Leaving the class with Mr Pitson, I set off in my car to look in the village centre where we were used to going with the children. I was lucky to flag down a passing police car and they took me with them – there was talk of police helicopters if we failed to find him. He was not in the village so we returned to school and there he was as large as life. He had been seen near the Bird in Hand pub by the parent of another child in the class and she brought him back. This was a child with a heart condition who we put in a buggy if we had to cover any distance. He calmly explained that he had felt poorly and decided to go home. He lived in Caversham and clearly knew where he was going. The policemen told him not to do it again but were not nearly fierce enough with him for my liking. I then had to telephone his parents who were amazingly understanding and told me that he had done a disappearing act from home in the past and been found near Waitrose. I wish I'd known that!!

We took part in as much of mainstream school life as we could including joining in with the 75th anniversary in 1988. Our decade covered the years of the second world war. The children enjoyed dressing up and carrying their gas mask boxes. This picture of Ruth and myself as Land Army girls is one of my favourites.

Land Army Girls

My second class comprised Steven Frankum, John Beville and Emily in the middle, Ellie, David and Katy Sunman at the front.

In 1990 I resumed my post in the mainstream school and in 1992 became Mr Pitson's deputy. It was a shock when he was offered and decided to take early retirement but the school governors asked me to take the role of acting headteacher for a term and I felt that, with the support of colleagues, (especially Pam Gibbon who was bursar/secretary) I could do it. The term was challenging but enjoyable and confirmed what I had always known, namely that I had no desire to become a headteacher permanently.

Mr Pip Marples became head in January 1993 and soon after that I took on the additional role of Special Needs Coordinator (SENCo). I was able to keep my close link with Bishopswood School and also look after the interests of the less able pupils and the more able pupils in the school. During the next ten years I taught classes throughout the school from Rising 5 to Year 5. One year, when the school had a favourable budget I did not have my own class but worked with groups of children, from the very able to the least able. That situation was never likely to last and eventually, I returned to the age group for which I had specifically trained and most enjoyed working with – Year 2. Working as a team with Mrs Lynda Hanks was great and having Mrs Jill Pound as our Key Stage Leader could not have been better.

Pip and I worked well as a team – he was a good starter and I was a good finisher – he always said. We had many challenges over the next 15 years including the arrival of SATs and OFSTED (several times). Pip led a cohesive team and when there were disagreements, he was a headteacher you could talk to and he usually listened. When personal tragedy struck in 1999 and my husband died suddenly, aged just 47, both staff and pupils helped me through and I returned to school as quickly as I could. Pip arranged for a trophy to be given in his name (Appendix 2) as he had helped with cricket coaching for a number of years.

This Christmas display owes much to Blue Peter – I often 'borrowed' their ideas for cards and calendars and the robins made from dried beech leaves has been used many times.

School Trips

In addition to innumerable day visits I enjoyed many residential trips. Enjoyed is probably best used retrospectively since at the time they are exhausting and at the end of a week with little sleep I would usually vow *'never again'* until the next time.

Trips to Woodlands in Glasbury-on-Wye with Year 6 were usually memorable and the one pictured here in 1995 was no exception. Mrs Hutchinson and myself (both in the back row) were the teachers on this trip but Woodlands is staffed by qualified teachers who have additional qualifications in outdoor activities. But they go off duty at about nine in the evening which is when the fun starts until the last night when the children are too tired to do anything but sleep. The adults are encouraged to take part in all the activities alongside their pupils. Abseiling, canoeing, hill walking, jungle gym, zip wire – no problem – but caving was not an experience to be enjoyed. I hated it, crawling on my stomach with the cave roof only inches away, being posted through the 'letterbox', wet, bruised, cold and in the dark with an unreliable head light. For a teacher used to being in control it was difficult to have no control at all and be totally reliant on the leader and when emerging from the cave in what feels like days later but is only a couple of hours to realise that the area covered is actually tiny. Apart from being character building I did not really get it. It did lead to one of my favourite moments in teaching, however. One of the pupils in my group was a boy called Michael with whom I often worked as he found some aspects of learning a challenge. He became my supporter in the cave and at the end he said to me-

'That was really good because usually you help me but today I was helping you.'

This trip to Swanage in 2002 was much more fun as you can see from my and Mrs Hems faces as we abseiled down the climbing wall.

South Oxfordshire schools quiz

In 1997 I started the South Oxfordshire Quiz competition which was sponsored by the Henley Standard. I wrote the questions, distributed them, collated the results and conducted the draw for each round. This continued until I left the school in 2009 and was not able to persuade any South Oxfordshire colleague to take it on. During these years, my own teams were twice the winners. In 2005 Jessica Mernagh captained the winning team with Laura Burgess, Andrew Lee and Daniel Houghton and in 2008 we triumphed again. I felt very proud of all my teams.

2005 Henley Standard

2008 winning team - Maddy Smith (captain), Christopher Humm,
Mrs White, Rowan Stacey, Caitlin Stacey

Sonning Common School is very special. It has a unique atmosphere of learning and support which has endured through many changes of leadership, staff and children. It was difficult to leave after 34 years continuous service but I had decided a number of years earlier that I would take early retirement in 2009 and so I did. I was surprised that Pip Marples beat me to it but it enabled me to work for two terms with Chris Hirst and help him in his new post.

During my time at the school I taught in almost all the rooms in both buildings, both HORSAs before they were demolished and the computer suite when it was still a classroom. I had classes across the age range from 4 to 11 and to confuse everyone, had three names, starting as Miss Mills, then Mrs Choules and finally, Mrs White as I married David in 2006.

This is my final class in September 2008. This is a lovely group of children – a really good way to finish.

Back row: Billy, Lucy, Ethan, Martyn, Max, Kyle, Lucy, Jessica, Phoebe, James, Charlie
Middle row: William, Maha, Bradley, Thomas, William, Katelyn, Tia, Joshua, Zara
Front row: Emily, Kittie, Samantha, Kyle, Billy, Ella, Ellie, Lewis, Olivia, Erin

This is a favourite picture from 2009 which shows the fun we had and the togetherness of the staff even in tricky conditions.

Mrs Thurlow, Mrs Mills, Mr Lovegrove, Mrs White, Mrs Hems, Miss Offer

Chapter Fourteen
A Caretaker's story – Patrick Butler

*P*at Butler became the caretaker in 1973 and is the longest serving member of staff in the history of the school. His family were in the caretaking business as his father had been a caretaker at Chiltern Edge School. In 1973 he was referred to as to as *"young"* Mr Butler in the Managers' Minutes. He remains caretaker to this day and is the first and only caretaker to live in the school house. Pat is the only person who has not been interviewed for this publication because he would almost certainly have refused to be included as he prefers to remain in the background.

He recalls the occasion when lead was stolen from the roof of the old hall (now library). It started to rain while the children were in assembly and he was summoned when water began to drip through. The teacher (probably Mr Pitson) said:

> *'I think there's a problem on the roof, Mr Butler'*

When Pat investigated he found the roof tiles stacked in neat piles. The police were called.

Mr Butler 2000

In turn, every headteacher has paid tribute to his hard work and dedication. He is always first on the scene whenever there is a problem with locks, lighting, lavatories or anything else from A to Z. He knows everything about the premises and, without him, there would be no swimming, no services and no security. Pat has been a stalwart of the Governors' Environment Committee for many years because no one knows the site better than him. He carries with him this set of keys which he says have barely changed in all his years of carrying them about. He is the only one who knows which lock each will fit. For many years he patrolled the grounds in the evenings with his dog, William for company as he made sure all doors and windows were locked and the swimming pool cleaned and ready for the next day.

In 1982, Mr Sharman said:

> *'I must pay tribute to Mr Pat Butler and Mr George Allum. In my 17 years of teaching I have never met two such dedicated caretakers who are so genuinely fond of children. Nothing has been too much trouble for these 2 gentlemen and the school is truly fortunate to have them.'*

During Mr Sharman's time they helped create a pond, an aviary, a small garden, a poultry unit and two greenhouses.

Of course, Pat has always insisted that he does not like children at all, nor teachers for that matter, but everyone knows that his bark is definitely worse than his bite and as Mr Pitson said-

> *'I reckon the school would have fallen down without him. He might moan a bit but he'll always do it!'*

A 1989 Logbook entry reads-

> *'Health and Safety Officer called this afternoon after a neighbour had phoned to complain about Mr Butler walking his dog around the grounds. This person has already complained about 'flies', 'rats', 'bonfires', 'children', 'public address system', 'undergrowth in the Dobinson paddock', 'my deputy, Mr Edwards', and now my caretaker – what will the man think of next!!'*

Pat's tasks over the years have been many – always on hand to collect a large Christmas tree for the foyer, move furniture and staging from one place to another, climb the highest ladder to put up displays and most especially, keep the school clean and maintained. With this task, he has been ably assisted by his wife Salvacion who he married in 1990. Here he is helping to get the hall ready for lunches in the days before benches were used.

1988 Pat at work

In 2003 Pat's quick actions averted a damaging fire when a pupil returning to his classroom after rugby club set fire to paper at the back of his classroom. Pat managed to put it out and then alerted staff who were meeting in another part of the building. He is the fire marshal and possibly the only person trained to use all the extinguishers and other equipment. He has always been in charge of fire alarms, deciding when the fire practice should be and which members of staff he would allow to know in advance.

In 2004 a pupil set off the fire alarm in the morning when Pat was off duty (and in town). Pat had the only key to switch it off.

There are few pictures of Pat but he was persuaded to pose in 2000 for the planting of an oak tree with Amy and Sarah Hart.

They say no one is irreplaceable but Patrick Butler comes close.

Chapter Fifteen
Mr C. Hirst 2009 – present

Mr Chris Hirst became headteacher in January 2009, having previously been head of Brill C of E Combined School in Buckinghamshire. The number of pupils on roll has been steadily increasing and is expected to top 400 by September 2012.

He was interviewed by the Henley Standard on appointment and said-

> *'Every child is good at something and it is the duty of the school to find out exactly what that is so that they can strive to do the best they can. I will be working closely with the community, staff, governors and parents. I will build upon the ethos that has been created in this happy, child-centred school to create an environment where I would want my own children to be educated, where only the best is good enough.'*

The year 2012 has been a great one for the school with the best ever set of Standard Attainment Tests (SATs) results. In addition, the team triumphed in a mathematics competition at Highdown School, Emmer Green which involved teams from Oxfordshire and Berkshire schools.

Spiralling costs

Over the last 100 years there have always been budgeting issues and it has never been too much money to spend but always too little. The budget has increased over time, however. In 1924 the annual cost of the school was reported as £1217 16s and in 2011-2012 as £1,390,984.

Values Education

Values education remains at the centre of school life. The original 5 values have been slightly changed in order to make them easier for children to understand and follow. Children, parents and everyone connected with the school were invited to vote on what the new values should be and it was decided that the core values should be:

Respect, Truth, Kindness, Politeness and Doing Your Best

Staff have already started to explain to pupils what the words mean and what they will mean for them within school. A system of coloured wrist bands which children can earn for demonstrating that they are adhering to the values has been introduced. It is hoped that they will apply the values to their everyday life in school and beyond. An annual Citizen Award has been introduced and a Values Cup for each year group in Key Stage 2 (Appendix 2).

Clubs and extra-curricular activities

The school continues to encourage pupils to take part in many activities outside the main curriculum. There is a before school running club, a netball club and a tag rugby club. The Pupils School Council and the Eco-Council are guided by members of staff. In addition, multi-sports, ballet, judo, swimming, forest camp, chess and mini bridge are available to the children.

Forest school (run by Mrs Phillippa Byrne) which gives children the chance to co-operate, work and learn together in an outdoor environment has been expanded to include children from different age groups.

Forest school

Mr Hirst is keen to support residential and day trips for pupils and to take part himself when he can.

Mr Hirst on a canoeing trip at Woodlands

This photograph of Mr Hirst's first staff group (2009) was also Mrs White's last so everyone was encouraged to be there.

Back row: Miss Pembroke, Mrs Humm, Mrs Stevenson, Mrs Rice, Mrs Byrne, Mrs Myhill, Mrs Doughty, Mrs Hinks, Mrs Bodenham, Mr Loader
Middle row: Mr Lovegrove, Mrs Byrne, Mrs Conway, Mrs Quinton, Mrs Green, Mrs Ashton, Miss Bartlett, Mrs Stowell, Mrs Room, Miss Price, Mrs Estcourt, Mrs Mills, Mrs Pound, Mrs Soden
Front row: Mrs Hanks, Mrs Thurlow, Miss Gordon, Miss Offer, Mrs Hems, Mr Hirst, Mrs White, Mrs Matthews, Miss Winton, Mrs Harris, Mrs John

Sport

The London 2012 Olympics have inspired the children to work even harder at their sports. The school arranged for many former Olympians and Paralympians to visit the school and talk about their experiences at the highest level of sporting achievement so when the Olympic flame passed through Nettlebed village, they wanted to be there, cheering it on with their imaginative posters.

Henley Standard

The school triumphed in a new competition, Quad Kids (throw, jump, sprint and 600m run) firstly in South Oxfordshire and then in the county overall. The indoor athletics team are County Champions and there have been great numbers competing in cross country running competitions bringing success to both individuals and teams.

The Centenary

Plans are underway to celebrate the school's centenary on January 6th 2013. There will be displays and Open Days, dressing up days, a time line and a fabulous mosaic contributed to by all the children.

A competition to design a centenary logo was won by Alice Jones. It is planned that this will be used to top all school communications in the centenary year.

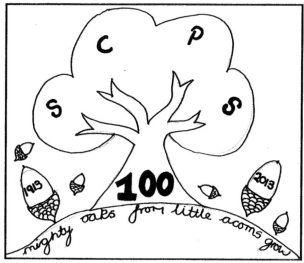

Alice's Winning Design

Everyone in the school gathered on the field for this 100 year celebratory photograph. The original 1913 buildings cannot be seen but many of the additions of the last 100 years are visible including the infant block, Bishopswood School, Year 6 classrooms, the swimming pool and the garden area which the younger children cultivate and harvest.

The final words of this first one hundred years of Sonning Common Primary School belong to the current headteacher, Mr Chris Hirst -

'As we look back over the past 100 years of our history at Sonning Common Primary School we also look forwards to the next 100. We look at the accomplishments of our ancestors with pride and maybe a few smiles and hope that we are able to emulate them, the smiles and the accomplishments. The past year, 2011-2012, has been an amazing year in terms of our sporting and academic achievements which overall seem to be one of the best ever years in our history. Our commitment to values education is as strong as it has ever been and our commitment to educate and develop the 'whole child' will always remain a priority for us all. All of these achievements have set us in the right direction. A new era awaits and we are ready for all of the challenges that we will surely face...'

Appendix 1: Junior Scholarship Examinations – 1921

Oxfordshire Education Committee
Junior Scholarship Examinations 1921

These are the papers children would be expected to take in order to gain a scholarship to Henley Grammar School in 1921. I wonder how we would fare with these today – at any age.

OXFORDSHIRE EDUCATION COMMITTEE.

County Junior Scholarship Examination.

19TH MARCH, 1921, 11.45–1.

Composition Paper.

[*You should answer either (a) or (b) of Question 1 and Question 2. Do not hurry your work. Think out clearly what you intend to say and write carefully.*]

1. Either, (a) Write a full and careful description of a bicycle.

Or, (b) If you were shipwrecked close to a desert island describe how you would reach land, how you would live, and how you would try to get away.

2. Write a sentence for each of the following words, using each word in its proper sense:—goal, gaol, alter, altar, respectful, respectable, wring, ring.

Composition paper

Appendix 1: cont.

County Junior Scholarship Examination.

19TH MARCH, 1921, 2–3.15.

English and General Paper.

1. Divide the following sentence into Subject and Predicate. Say what part of speech each word underlined is, and give your reasons.

' I often visit Oxford to see its famous buildings.'

2. Rewrite these sentences correctly :—

(a) Me and him is to sing that song.

(b) The river has flown over its banks.

(c) Through loosing her book Mary cannot work her sums right.

(d) Some boy or other have tied this knot wrong.

3. Make five sentences, using each of the following words as nouns :—light, knock, sleep, shouting, round.

4. Write a few lines on *three* only of the following persons :—Becket, Joan of Arc, Francis Drake, Wolfe, Nelson, Lord Kitchener, Lord Falkland.

5. Write short answers to *two* of the following :—

(a) What happens inside the bicycle pump when you pump up a bicycle tyre ?

(b) How, when, and in what kind of soil would you plant potatoes to secure a good crop ?

(c) Mary cuts her finger badly. What should she do to try and heal it quickly ?

(d) What causes a fog ?

(e) Write the history of a piece of chalk.

6. From what parts of the world do we get the following goods :—cotton, wheat, rice, rubber, wood (for matches, doors, &c.) ?

208

English and General paper

OXFORDSHIRE EDUCATION COMMITTEE.

County Junior Scholarship Examination.

19th March, 1921. 10—11.30.

Arithmetic.

[*All working must be clearly shown on the paper. Give the number of each question, and leave a clear space between each worked sum.*]

1. How many half-crown books can be bought with £59. 7s. 6d. ?

2. Subtract eight thousand eight hundred and eight from fifteen thousand and fifteen.

3. If 10 cotton reels contain 1 mile of cotton, how many inches of cotton are there on each reel ?

4. In a village there are 145 families, each family containing 3 children. If each child is given a halfpenny, how much is given altogether ?

5. How many hours are there in the month of March ?

6. A man buys provisions to last him 4 months. They would last a friend of his 6 months. If the 2 men lived together, how long would these provisions last them ?

7. An acre of land is cut up in 11 equal plots, each being 37½ yds. long. How wide was each plot ?

8. A shepherd sells a quarter of his flock, then loses 30 per cent. of the remainder, and finds he has 384 sheep left. How many sheep had he at first ?

9. Two friends stayed at a hotel, one for 8 days and the other for 9 days. The bill for the two came to £8. 12s. 1½d. How much should each pay of this ?

10. Add together 7·675, 51·375 and 105·5, and divide the result by ·35.

11. A piece of work will take 200 hours to complete. If a man works 6 hours 15 min. a day, and receives 10s. a day, how much will he have earned by the time the work is finished ?

206

Arithmetic paper

Appendix 2: Class Photographs 1969

Headmaster Mr Johnson preserved this set of class photographs from 1969. There is one class with no teacher and two teachers that have not been identified.

Mr Pitson's class

Mrs Bean's class

Mrs Jones class

Mrs Carter's class

Mrs Long's class

Mrs Evans class

Mrs Abbey's class

Miss Henessey-Law's class

Miss Day's class

Mr Beadle's class

Mr Henderson's class

Mrs Paddick's class

Appendix 2: Class Photographs 1969 cont.

Mr Roper's class

Mr Carter's class

Appendix 3: Trophy Winners

Trophy winners
The school has, since its early days, awarded trophies to pupils who achieved highly in different ways.

The Geoffrey Norris Trophy
Given by his parents and schoolfellows in loving memory of G Norris.

Died 11th May 1957, Aged 14

Sportsman of the Year

1958 D. Silcox	1959 D. Woods	1960 C. Figzal
1961 P. Howells	1962 B. Farr	1963 S. Howells
1964 J. Hayes, S. Gillett	1965 W. Cooke	1966 R. McIntosh
1967 R. Stansbury	1968 P. Borrett	1969 H. Jones
1970 Simon Wright	1971 Adam Simmonds	1972 Jeremy Cookson
1973 S. Szymans	1974 J. Cooke	1975 David Edwards
1976 M. Wenham	1977 M. Underwood	1978 Dave Stevens
1979 Gary Lambourne	1980 Simon Pollard	1981 Martin Smith
1982 John Palmer	1983 Mark Lambourne	1984 Mark Treadwell
1985 David Best	1986 Peter Hayden	1987 Guy Palmer, James Howles
1988 Andrew Leaver	1989 Martin Chandler	1990 David Low, David Watkins
1991 Stuart Moss	1992 James Hancock	

Appendix 3 cont.

The Frank Lockwood Trophy
Honoured master 1938 – 1958
Sportswoman of the Year

1966 S. Bowker	1967 Marion Carter	1968 Corina West
1969 Wendy Wise	1970 Catherine Wing	1971 Katherine Jeffery
1972 Shona Tantum	1973 Jacqueline Bussell	1974 Kate Martel
1975 Diana Cooke	1976 Sarah Wallace	1977 Claire Foxley
1978 Louise Morgan	1979 Karen Pollard	1980 Jackie Farina
1981 Sally Cutts	1982 Michelle Brennan	1983 Alison Lee
1984 Clare Mills	1985 Graina Mullins	1986 Laura Porteous
1987 Joanne Smith, Ann-Marie Smith	1988 Louise Coy	1989 Caroline Orr, Katie Sharp
1990 Marieke Tyldesley, Amanda Watkins	1991 Frances Howson, Bethany Griffin	1992 Naomi Readings

Guide Dog award for Service to the Community
(donated by Mrs Sue Badnell)

1990 Donna Clark	1991 Claire Green	1992 Lindsey Blodwell
1993 Joanna Waugh, Emma McGill	1994 Lisa Tilbury	1995 Fleur Holmes
1996 Nicola Pitt, Thomas Borrett,	1997 Graham Laurence	1998 Holly Shillito, Thomas Rockell
1999 Elizabeth Maul	2000 Laura Neighbour, Verity Cottrell	2001 Grant Readings, Laura Richards
2002 Oliver Yarrow, Andrew Bulpitt	2003 Samantha Hayward	2004 Sophie Warren
2005 Anna McLean, Molly Kirby	2006 Jamie Lindsay	2007 Catherine Hill
2008 Emma Dawson	2009 Archie McGowan	2010 Charlotte van Walwyk
2011 Hamzah Hussain		

Progress Cup

(donated by Mrs Sari Stacey)

1995 Matthew Aylward

1996 Charlie Knapp

1997 Carl Bennett

1998 Kathryn Tunmore

1999 Jade Gordon

2000 Dominic O'Reilly

2001 Samuel Hargreaves

2002 John and Tom Woodley

2003 Abbie Greaves

2004 Samuel Grindey

2005 Sophie Burling

2006 Duncan Andrews

2007 Alfie Ireland,
Miles Pennie

2008 Wiktor Parzyszek

2009 Laurie Martin

2010 Freya Leith

2011 James Rhodes,
Lauryn Challis

2012 Owen Attree

Roger Choules Cricket Cup

1999 Freddie Kirby

2000 Fergus Adamson

2001 Joseph Matthews

2002 Catherine Davison,
Stewart Davison

2003 Thomas Kelly

2004 Elody Fumi,
Thomas Kelly

2005 Matthew Thomas

2006 Kayla Jenkins

2008 Matthew Slater

2009 Rowan Stacey

2010 Jonathan Abbott

2011 Daniel Jordan

2012 Jack Stevens

Kayla Jenkins Girls Cricket Cup

2008 Emily Estcourt

2009 Charlie Estcourt

2010 Lily Stevens

2011 Rhian Ramsey

2012 Amber Bellamy

Appendix 3 cont.

Governors' Cup for Academic Achievement

2004-5 Jessica Mernagh
2005-6 Louisa Carlisle, Sarah Barker
2006-7 Laura Burgess
2007-8 Amy Lovell
2008-9 India Burgess
2009-10 Marcus Pike
2010-11 Isabel Mulligan, Caitlin Stacey
2011-12 Fred Newbold

Mr Marples Music Cup

2009 Bryony Floyd
2010 Christopher Humm
2011 Alice Jones
2012 Max White

Swimming Trophy

2011 Henry Bell
2012 Francesca Perkins

Citizen Award

2012 Ellie Underwood, Martyna Brzana

Values Cup Year 6

2012 Archie Scobey

Values Cup Year 5

2012 Thomas Capaldi

Values Cup Year 4

2012 Lucinda Elwell

Values Cup Year 3

2012 Nickola Symolon

Appendix 4: The 100 photograph

The 100 Year photograph was taken by Alan Ney piloted by Rob Bentata. Everyone in school that day is in the picture. The sequence of getting all the children into place before the plane came over is shown here.

Rob Bentata – pilot

Alan Ney - photographer

The children file out.

The formation takes shape.

The 100 is created.

Bibliography

The Education of the People Mary Sturt
PUB- BUTLER AND TANNER LTD, LONDON 1967

A Little World Apart Jill Kendal
PUB 2000

Rural Life in South Oxfordshire 1841-1891 Sonning Common WEA
PUB 1994

A personal story of Oxfordshire Primary Schools 1946-1956 Edith Moorhouse
PUB 1985 E MOORHOUSE

An Introductory History of English Education since 1800
S J Curtis and M E A Boultwood
PUB UTP LTD 1960

The Victorian and Edwardian Schoolchild Pamela Horne
ALAN SUTTON PUBLISHING 1989

Amid the Dancing Shadows Ruth Mason
TROUBADOR PUBLISHING 2009

Goring School - The First 150 Years Michael Anderson
PUB 2005 PIE POWDER PRESS

Thanks

Many people have helped with this publication by providing pictures, photographs, names and anecdotes. There are too many to mention individually but I have tried to include something from all of them by way of thanks.

Particular thanks are due to the following:

Caroline Conway: support and additional research

Alan Ney and **Rob Bentata**: aerial 100 photograph

Robert Mills: advice

Rosemary Dunstan and **Sue Mills**: proofreading

David White: support, advice and proofreading

Acknowledgements

Henley Standard: permission to use any of their pictures and articles

Tempest Photography: permission to use school photographs

Sponsors

We are grateful to the following who have sponsored this publication financially:

Sonning Common Parish Council

Oak Grove Garden Services

Peppard Building Supplies

Davis Tate Estate Agents